# BETWEEN
# THE MOUNTAINS

## A PORTRAIT OF EASTERN WASHINGTON

Northwest Geographer™ Series

Number 1

by John A. Alwin

**Northwest Panorama Publishing, Inc.**
**Box 1858   Bozeman, MT 59771**

Library of Congress Catalog Card Number: 84-61945

ISBN 0-9613787-0-0

**Production credits**

Design and Layout: Ann Alwin, B.F.A.
               Bozeman, Montana

Cover and
Technical Advice: Mark Thibeault
               Thibeault Graphics
               Bozeman, Montana

Typesetting:  Color World of Montana
               Bozeman, Montana

Cartography:  Cecelia R. Vaniman, A.I.A.
               Bozeman, Montana

Color Lithography:  Dai Nippon
               San Francisco

Printed in Japan

**The Cover**

Right: Mader brother heads for the field on the family's Palouse farm. Upper left: Fall color in the Yakima Valley. Lower left: Spokane skyline from the South Hill. Middle: Columbia National Wildlife Refuge. John Alwin photos

**Title page**

Golden waves of grain near Ritzville. John Alwin photo

**Contents page**

Columbia National Wildlife Refuge. John Alwin photo

**About This Series**

For its size, the Northwest is one of the world's most diverse regions. Few can rival its kaleidoscope of history, natural landscapes, climates, geology, urban centers, economic activity, and peoples. A geographer couldn't ask for a more interesting study area.

Each profusely illustrated and highly readable *Northwest Geographer*™ will focus on one component region or a specific Northwest topic. This captivating series is designed for the geographer in each of us and especially for the justifiably proud residents fortunate enough to call this special place home.

To be added to the *Northwest Geographer*™ Series mailing list and receive information on pre-publication discounts on future books, write:

Northwest Panorama Publishing Inc.
*NORTHWEST GEOGRAPHER* Series
P.O. Box 1858
Bozeman, MT 59771

## FOREWORD

My introduction to Eastern Washington dates to August 1968, when I flew into Spokane and then caught an old Hughes Air West flight to Pullman to begin a graduate program in geology. I had to arrive on campus early since all graduate students were required to participate in a field trip across Eastern Washington and into the North Cascades. At the time I didn't realize it, but as our small caravan headed out of Pullman west across the Palouse, I was beginning an odyssey, an intimate relationship with Eastern Washington, which has now grown to almost two decades.

My 1970 marriage to fellow student and Ellensburger, Ann Marsh, guaranteed periodic trips back across the region to visit family. These two- to three-times annual crossings served to pique my interest in this fascinating, big open country.

Two years ago I began in-earnest research for this book. It involved over 10,000 miles of criss-crossing the region via most of its paved highways as well as many of its more challenging "local inquiry advised" roadways. I visited with scores of residents from farmers and migrants, to university professors, mayors, soldiers, Indians, and countless others. During my wandering I took more than 5,000 slides.

My objective was straightforward, to paint a verbal and visual picture of the land and people of this often misunderstood and stereotyped corner of Washington.

# CONTENTS

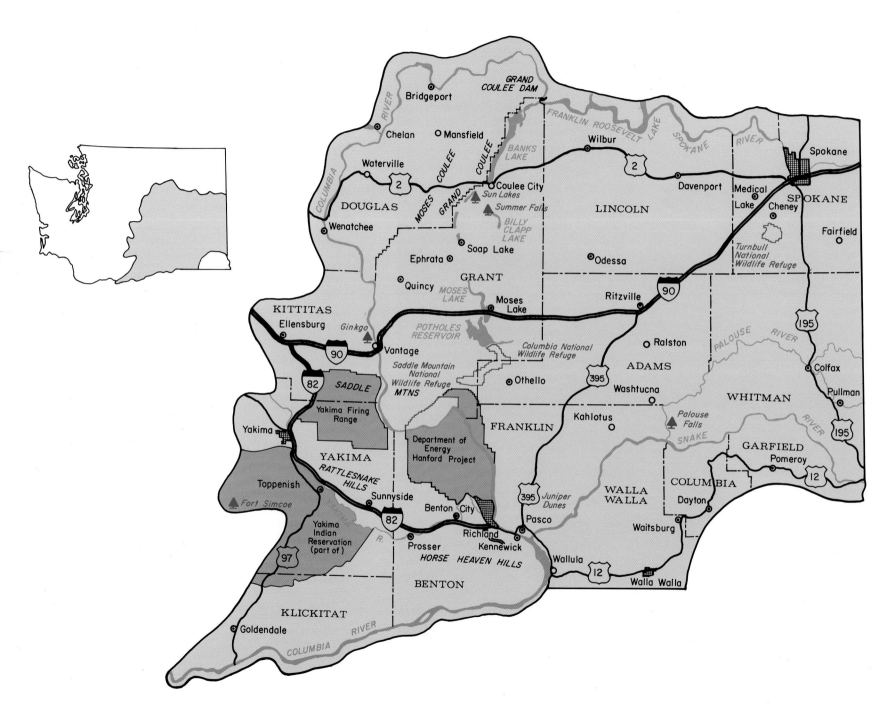

*The region defined, Washington between the mountains.*

# A REGIONAL IDENTITY

## Between the Mountains

*Harvest time in the Palouse. John Alwin photo*

Driving Interstate 90 or U.S. Highway 2 east-west across the Evergreen State travellers do not cross a wide yellow line announcing that they have just entered or left Eastern Washington. Such a demarcation would be impossible, since there is not just one Eastern Washington. Its limits depend on who is defining it and on the criteria used. In this geography, Eastern Washington corresponds to the section of Washington between the foothills of the Cascade Range on the west, Okanogan Highlands on the north, Idaho line to the east, and the Blue Mountains and Oregon border on the south. Physical geographers know this area between the mountains as Washington's section of the Columbia Basin landform region.

Of late, the state's travel promotion unit has been billing the Evergreen State as the "Other Washington." Ours is the other Washington's other Washington. East of the Cascades and within the Columbia Basin is a big and open country. It isn't as three-dimensional as many other sections of

the state, and yet the land looms large and its basalt-dominated geology lies exposed. This is the dry, brown and sage-toned side of the state, with some parched sections meriting desert designation. Its 900,000 people seem to have a different sense of distance than their west-side cousins; rural residents think nothing of driving 100 miles round trip for a Friday night movie. Eastern Washington is agricultural Washington, accounting for almost 90 percent of the state's cropland and responsible for the lion's share of its agricultural products. The region has a well-developed small town and rural flavor, and yet less than 10 percent live on farms, with many more residing in the region's three metropolitan areas.

Eastern Washington is easily the most misunderstood part of the state, perhaps in part because it has not received the same widespread exposure of its western counterpart. It is a section that merits closer inspection by residents and non-residents alike. Those who explore Washington between the mountains will find a special place with its own beauty and personality. Those who take the time to look will discover a surprising diversity of land and people.

A

B

C

G

E

D

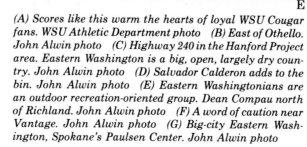

F

(A) Scores like this warm the hearts of loyal WSU Cougar fans. WSU Athletic Department photo   (B) East of Othello. John Alwin photo   (C) Highway 240 in the Hanford Project area. Eastern Washington is a big, open, largely dry country. John Alwin photo   (D) Salvador Calderon adds to the bin. John Alwin photo   (E) Eastern Washingtonians are an outdoor recreation-oriented group. Dean Compau north of Richland. John Alwin photo   (F) A word of caution near Vantage. John Alwin photo   (G) Big-city Eastern Washington, Spokane's Paulsen Center. John Alwin photo

*(A) Cowboy country, the Ellensburg Rodeo. John Alwin photo   (B) Big rivers and hydro power dams like Lower Granite on the Snake are synonymous with Eastern Washington. U.S. Army Corps of Engineers   (C) Local farmers, Warren and Howard Morris avail themselves of the perennial pot of coffee at Sara Goude's Country Store in Hooper. John Alwin photo   (D) A traditional Indian tepee suits Ken Scabbyrobe and his son while at the Yakima Indian days. John Alwin photo   (E) Abandoned Krenz farmstead west of Wilbur. John Alwin photo   (F) After bass on the Potholes Reservoir. John Alwin photo   (G) Ubiquitous basalt, the regional rock. John Alwin photo*

# THE PHYSICAL BASE
## A GEOLOGIC LEGACY

*Basalt layers and talus slope near Vantage take on a red tinge in the late afternoon sun. John Alwin photo*

Eastern Washingtonians live within one of the most unique geologic provinces in all of North America. Because of its distinctiveness, this area is known world-wide by geologists. Its rocks and surface features tell a fascinating story of times when lush, almost subtropical forests thrived, when firey lava issued forth from deep within the bowels of the earth, and when gargantuan floods ripped across the landscape. Geology not only explains much of the terrain we see today, it also helps us understand the patterns of other features, from scenic wonders to climate, agriculture, and recreational attractions.

If we go back about 16 million years to the time of the Miocene epoch, we can consider some of the geologic factors that helped shape the region and produce the rocks and other features we now see at and near the surface. Back then Eastern Washington probably had a landscape that ranged from rolling and even mountainous terrain, to sections with gentle relief. Since there was no blocking Cascade Range to the west, moisture-laden air wafting in off the Pacific gave the region a humid climate that supported a rich and diversified land with extensive forests and swamps, and abundant rivers and lakes.

The relative tranquility of verdant mid-Miocene Eastern Washington was soon to be shaken. Because of the build-up of deep-seated stress in the earth below the region, floods of molten basaltic lava began welling up through giant fissures in the earth's crust. In what must have been awesome spectacles, glowing lava flowed outward, destroying all life in its path, engulfing forests,

*Tilted basalt layers rise 600 feet above the surrounding terrain to form Gable Mountain at the north end of the Hanford Project. Facilities atop the barren highland are associated with a series of tunnels mined into the mountain's side to test the thermal and mechanical properties of basalt. U.S. Dept. of Energy photo*

blocking rivers, and remaking the landscape. This was exceptionally fluid lava. Instead of piling up into cones or volcanoes, each flow spread laterally, often with a remarkably uniform thickness.

Initial flows, like flood waters, first filled low areas in the landscape, thus the name, "flood basalts." Successive outpourings piled on top in layer-cake fashion as chronicled on the walls of the region's deeply cut river valleys. In the eastern section, near the Idaho border, where the mid-Miocene terrain may have been most mountainous, the summits of the highest peaks are thought to have remained as islands in an engulfing sea of lava. Today these basalt-free areas are known as steptoes, after prominent Steptoe Butte north of Colfax.

Volcanic activity continued intermittently for at least seven million years, although most flows were extruded in the initial three million. By the beginning of the succeeding Pliocene epoch, approximately five million years ago, flows had buried Eastern Washington and adjacent sections of Oregon and Idaho under thousands of feet of black basalt. Geologists collectively know these Miocene flows as the Columbia River basalts and have calculated they now cover 50,000 square miles with a minimum volume of about 25,000 cubic miles. Imagine the extent of the field before the effects of millions of years of erosion. The lava flood once may have covered an area at least twice as large, some suggest at depths great enough to bury even the steptoes.

Individual basalt flows average 70 or 80 feet thick, but range from a few feet to 300 feet in thickness. Since the lava was so fluid when reaching the surface, it travelled great distances before congealing. The distinctive Roza Member is one of the most studied flows. Evidence suggests the major part of this 100-foot-thick unit was extruded through a linear swarm of fissures in extreme Eastern Washington. Today the flow can be traced over an area of 8,800 square miles reaching almost to Spokane, beyond Ephrata and Quincy, and as far down the Columbia as The Dalles. The 160 cubic miles in this one horizontal volcanic unit equal more than six times the volume of the volcanic pile of rocks that makes up nearby, towering Mount Rainier.

*Above: Pancake-like layers of basalt tower above Banks Lake at Steamboat Rock State Park, dwarfing water recreationists. John Alwin photo*
*Right: Columbia River basalts today. Modified after U.S. Geological Survey Bulletin 1309*

Intervals of quiet between lava outpourings sometimes lasted thousands, if not tens of thousands, of years. This was sufficient time in some cases for soils to develop and vegetation to take root on these initially barren and bleak surfaces. Soils covered by subsequent flows remain as compacted and baked horizons sandwiched between basalt, and abundant petrified trees along bottoms of flows verify the presence of forests.

Fossil flora provide important clues to Miocene Eastern Washington. Numerous tree species have been identified including ginkgo and cyprus. Since the Cascades did not exist, the area opened westward to the moderating effect and moisture of the Pacific. With abundant precipitation and rivers periodically dammed by basalt flows, lakes and swamps were common.

In most parts of the world petrified forests are associated with sedimentary rocks, since molten igneous rocks (like basalt) normally ignite and destroy any vegetation they contact. Water was

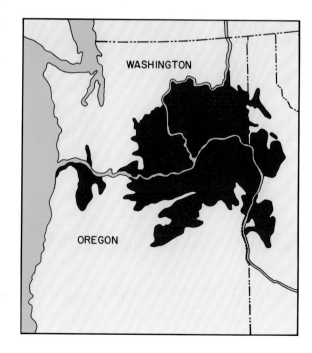

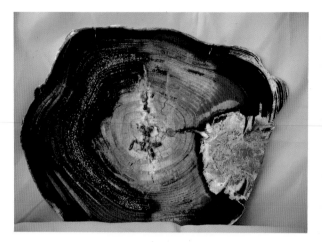

key to the preservation of Central Washington forests. The abundance of basalt pillow structures, bulbous surface forms associated with lava chilled quickly underwater, attest to the presence of water at the time of entombment.

Colorful petrified wood in association with basalt flows is found in western parts of the Columbia Basin. It once provided Indians with material for arrowheads and today is used by residents as an attractive landscaping rock for driveways and gardens. Washington's most famous and prolific location for petrified wood is Ginkgo Petrified Forest State Park at Vantage, where more than 200 species of trees have been identified. This area owes its richness to nearly ideal conditions for entombment and the fact that it includes both trees that were growing in the area and others rafted into Miocene Lake Vantage.

The Vantage forests and others recorded in basalt within a radius of about 75 miles have been named the Russell forests in honor of pioneer geologist, I. C. Russell. The Saddle Mountains is another plentiful area for fossil wood, although petrified wood can be found at the base of many flows over a wide area. At one place on the Columbia River a large petrified tree sticking out between flows halfway up the enclosing 250-foot-high wall of basalt was a landmark, of sorts. For 19th century Hudson's Bay Company employees passing in their bateaus, and for other early river travellers, it became a mile marker and object for target practice.

The Russell forests include both upright stumps and logs denuded of all limbs and bark. Rooted stumps represent trees that were growing in place. Species identified from petrified wood suggest that a humid swamp forest not unlike today's American Southeast covered the area during the Miocene. Take a midsummer, high noon stroll at Vantage and try to imagine swamps in place of sand, cyprus growing where sage now stands— that was mid-Miocene Vantage. Trees from different habitats, like cooler clime sequoia, were rafted in by rivers, stripped of bark and limbs enroute, and probably were water-logged and submerged in a shallow lake when the lava advanced. Spreading speed of some basalt flows has been estimated at a rapid 25 to 30 miles per hour. The firey advances of molten material into the area meant quick entombment. For some logs, rooted swamp trees, and other plants growing in bottomland there was sufficient water to protect them from burning. Once encased in basalt the magic process of petrification began with silica replacing wood, pore space by pore space, thus preserving in stone the structural detail of the wood, sometimes complete with worm burrows. At Ginkgo visitors can walk along trails where tree stumps turned to stone and were locked in basalt for millions of years before being exposed for viewing. Basin Indians knew of the petrified wood and attributed it to the supernatural powers of Coyote, the greatest of the animal people. According to legend he changed the forest to stone out of spite.

Evidence of lakes on the Miocene landscape can be read in other deposits wedged between flows. In the western part of the Basin, layers of siltstone, sandstone, and conglomerates of the Ellensburg Formation are lithified sediments, some with fossil freshwater snails and clams, that accumulated on lake bottoms and along the rivers that fed them. Several thick, white diatomite beds, formed by shells of single-celled plants that piled up on the bottom of Miocene lakes, now contrast with dark basalt rock above and below.

In the Spokane area, along the basalt field's eastern margin, advancing lava flows interrupted drainage. Streams flowing off the Rockies' west slope were dammed, ponding water into local lakes and swamps. Leaves found in bottom sediments of mud and clay, now hardened into rock called the Latah Formation, are among the world's best preserved Miocene plant fossils. Most college historical geology texts mention these famous fossils, known to many Spokane area school kids.

The thick deposits have yielded exceptionally detailed impressions of complete leaves of a wide range of species including ginkgo, cyprus, sequoia, oak, elm, maple, poplar, and magnolia. Some ginkgo leaves are so well preserved they can be removed intact and mounted between glass plates for display. The shale also includes impressions of acorns and other fruits and berries. As well as being of interest in their own right, like other fossils found between basalt flows, they help date eruptions.

11

Left: This towering basalt colonnade was a roadside landmark before Interstate 90 diverted traffic out of the Frenchman Springs cataract. John Alwin photo

Bottom left: Geometrical columns exposed from above at a roadcut in Grand Coulee south of Sun Lakes State Park. John Alwin photo

Bottom right: A familiar sight to Spokanites travelling to and from the airport, these classic columns look as though they could have been chiseled by a sculptor. John Alwin photo

# BASALT COLUMNS
## Devil's Fenceposts

The lava flows of the Columbia Basin oozed from the earth at temperatures of 1000° to 1200°C, hot enough to cast a warm glow on even the most distant "on-lookers." Many spread great distances, some at impressive speeds. Once flows stopped, basalt did not instantaneously cool and solidify. In fact, it may have taken decades for thicker flows to crystallize. The cooling process proceeded inward from both the top and bottom of the flow and in many cases produced distinctive features still visible today.

Basalt columns, or columnar basalt, is easily the most eye-catching of these cooling features. If you saw the film, "Close Encounters of the Third Kind," you saw actor Richard Dreyfus build a living-room size version of Devil's Tower and then scratch vertical lines on its sides—these were columnar joints. If you missed the movie but have driven across Eastern Washington, chances are almost certain you have seen well-developed columns in basalt outcrops. Characteristically, columns are vertical with parallel sides, but some curve

or have fan-like orientations. Individual columns are geometrical in cross section, typically with five or six sides, and may be anywhere from less than a foot across to several feet in diameter. Columns may range up to 20, 40, or 60 or more feet tall.

Basalt columns are directly related to the cooling history of each flow. When lava cools, it contracts, and shrinkage cracks (joints) commonly develop perpendicular to the cooling surfaces. Like three-dimensional mud cracks, columns tend toward hexagons, one of nature's preferred shapes. Typically one flow will have two or three distinct layers of jointing which can give the appearance of two or three different flows. The largest and best-developed columns are found in the top and bottom layers, the upper and lower colonnade which cooled most quickly. Between these tiers there may be an entablature in which columns are both smaller and more irregular. Some units have such unique colonnade-to-entablature relationships that these cooling features can be used to help identify and correlate flows in the field.

*Above left: The chimney-like Two Sisters landmark south of Wallula is comprised of two sections of entablature and an underlying colonnade. John Alwin photo*
*Above: Layer-cake basalt and detail of the two colonnades and entablature of one flow. John Alwin photo*

13

The most unique fossil discovered in the basalts of Eastern Washington is the Blue Lake rhino. This small rhinoceros apparently was floating in a shallow lake in the lower end of what is now Grand Coulee when it was trapped in an advancing basalt flow. Cooled by water and mud, the molten lava did not instantaneously incinerate the animal. Instead, part of the rhino's impression was faithfully cast into the encasing basalt. Curiously, when discovered in 1935, the basalt cavity still contained several teeth and numerous bone fragments.

Exceptional circumstances like those that captured the rhino in rock were rare, and basalt-dominated Eastern Washington yields precious few fossils of the vertebrates that are assumed to have roamed the region between eruptions. Readers interested in visiting the site of this unique fossil should stop by the store at Laurent's Sun Village Resort about two miles south of Sun Lakes State Park. Earl and Carol Laurent are happy to direct visitors to the nearby small cave containing the cast.

Geologic evidence strongly suggests the saucer-like structure of the Columbia Basin, with peripheral elevations of 2,000 feet and higher dropping to less than 400 feet in the center near the Tri-Cities, had begun to form during the outpouring of Miocene lavas. In general, extensive flows are thinnest around the Basin's outer edge and thicker toward the center. Even though the Roza Member surfaced through a narrow vent system that extended from just west of Spokane southeasterly through the extreme corner of the state, only a small volume of lava advanced eastward before being stopped by the uphill slope. Most of the Roza spread to the west toward the subsiding center of the Basin where it achieved the greatest thickness.

The sheer weight of the thickening, multi-layered pile, coupled with the withdrawal of magma and resultant loss of underlying support, caused the earth's crust to sink, or sag, and partly explains the existence of today's Columbia Basin. Wells that have reached through the thickest parts of the basalt field are rare, but the few that have document the massive volume of these combined flows. Three natural gas wells drilled near Ellensburg showed a basalt depth of more than one mile. Farther east toward the assumed center of the Basin the pile is even thicker. In the late Fifties one well in Benton County penetrated more than two miles of basalt and still hadn't punched through this thick volcanic layer. In 1984 a well atop the Saddle Mountains reached a state record depth of 17,518 feet. The depth at which this "tight hole" broke through the basalt has not been released. Spokesmen for Shell Oil will now only say it was "more than 10,000 feet."

Eastern Washington's basin-like surface also can be linked to upwarping of surrounding areas. This was most dramatic when the Cascade Range began rising during the Pliocene epoch (approximately 5 million to 1.8 million years ago), dragging up adjacent basalt layers on the Basin's western slope. Analysis of plant fossils from early Pliocene deposits shows the continuation of a humid environment, suggesting the most dramatic arching of the Cascades and the resultant rainshadow occurred later.

The Pliocene was a time of less frequent and less voluminous lava outpourings. Lake and river sediments, some including volcanic sands and gravels shed into adjacent sections of Eastern Washington by the rising Cascades, cover sections in the central and western portions. This was a period when the thick basalt layers and associated sedimentary strata were deformed and eroded as nature worked at reshaping the land.

Structural deformation along the Basin's western margin, begun by at least late Miocene time, intensified during the Pliocene. North-south compressing forces gradually buckled basalt layers into striking, wave-like ridges (anticlines) and valleys (synclines) extending easterly from the Cascades between the valley of the Columbia River north to the Wenatchee Valley. Their names have a familiar ring to locals, including the Horse Heaven Hills, Rattlesnake Hills, Saddle Mountains, Frenchman Hills, Manastash Ridge, and the intervening valleys like the Yakima, Selah, Wenas, Kittitas, and Royal Slope.

Some of these Yakima Folds, as this series of anticlines is called, rose extremely slowly. So slowly, in fact, that in some places the Yakima and Columbia rivers were able to maintain their

*Completion rig for testing Yakima Canyon wildcat well. Jack Pyle, Shell Oil Company photo*

courses right across the rising structures, with downward cutting of the rivers keeping pace with the lifting of the anticlines. This is best seen along the Yakima River between Ellensburg and Yakima. Prior to the rise of the anticlines between the sites of these two cities, the river had established a meandering course, suggesting a somewhat lazy stream flowing across an area of low slope or even a level plain. In spite of the uplift of four major anticlines (Manastash, Umtanum, Yakima, and Selah) athwart this reach of the river, the Yakima was able to maintain its previous winding course, entrenching it into now deep and spectacular Yakima Canyon. Rather than following the river through these bisected anticlines like the older Yakima Canyon road (designated a Scenic Highway by the state), new Interstate 82 to the east takes freeway travellers on a roller-coaster ride up and down the folds.

# WISHPOOSH AND COYOTE

Geologists may call upon rising anticlines and down-cutting by the river to explain the Yakima's deep and spectacular canyon between Ellensburg and Yakima, but Indian legend provides a more colorful explanation linked to giant animal people of mythical time. Like many Indians in North America, those of the Columbia Basin believed that before humans were created the world was inhabited by a race of animal people. In mythology gigantic Beaver, Crow, Fox, and other creatures assumed both animal and human qualities. They usually had animal form, but could reason and speak. Among Basin tribes none could rival Coyote for his powers and exploits.

In one version of a famous legend a gigantic Beaver monster, named Wishpoosh, lived in Lake Cle Elum, a Cascades lake west of Ellensburg. Wishpoosh was sizable even by animal people standards and used his great size and lethal talons to jealously guard the lake's abundant fish for his own consumption. Animal people who tried to take fish were drowned and sometimes became a meal for Wishpoosh. Cut off from this important food source the animal people, in desperation, turned to Coyote.

Coyote agreed to render assistance but had heard of Beaver's great size and strength and knew his task would be difficult. He fashioned a large spear, attached it to himself with a cord and confronted the monster. A pitched battle of gargantuan proportions began immediately and in the fracus Coyote speared the behemoth Beaver. So great was the force of the battle royal that a trench was cut in solid rock as the combatants moved out of the lake and down the east slope. Water from the lake followed them, filling the channel as it was gouged, forming the Yakima River. To this day between Ellensburg and Yakima the deep Yakima Canyon traces their path.

*Spectacular Yakima Canyon between Ellensburg and Yakima, a favorite for floaters and fishermen.*
*John Alwin photo*

North of Vantage the Columbia River maintained its course across the rising Frenchman Hills where it now flows through that anticline through an unnamed water gap. Just downstream below Wanapum Dam, it has sliced through the Saddle Mountains via even deeper, 2,000-foot Sentinel, or Beverly, Gap. Some geologists think from here the ancestral Columbia may have flowed to the southwest, meeting its present course near The Dalles via Satus Pass and Goldendale. The rising Yakima Folds, in particular the extensive Horse Heaven Hills, evidently blocked this former course and diverted the river to a more easterly course. Eventually the river cut through that anticline at Wallula Gap, or Gateway, a gaping 1,200-foot-deep opening.

The mighty Columbia not only had to adjust to the rising Yakima Folds. Its route and that of its Spokane River tributary undoubtedly had different pre-basalt courses. Between Spokane and Wenatchee the Columbia-Spokane waterway now roughly traces the northern edge of the basalt field, having been pushed and shoved to its fringing course by a succession of northward spreading basalt flows.

As anticlines rose in the Yakima Folds, subsidence of major basins just to the east accelerated. The sagging Quincy Basin north of the Frenchman Hills, linear Othello Basin between that highland and the Saddle Mountains, and the extensive Pasco Basin between that anticline and the Horse Heaven Hills became centers for accumulation of sediments. Clay, silt, sand, and gravel from streams and periodic lakes which covered them became even more widespread in the following Pleistocene epoch.

# BURIED TREASURES

Plain, ordinary basalt, an unlikely winner in a rock beauty contest, is the earth's most abundant volcanic rock. The enormous pile that makes up the Columbia River basalt field of Eastern Washington and adjacent parts of Idaho and Oregon has a volume measured in terms of tens of thousands of cubic miles. It constitutes one of the world's largest continental basalt sheets, ranking behind India's Deccan flows, the Parana basalts of Brazil and Paraguay, and the Lake Superior Keweenawan basalts. Unfortunately for residents of the Pacific Northwest, their thick stack of rock does not hold commercial mineral treasures like diamonds, gold, silver, or even copper, lead, or zinc. Still, this extraordinarly abundant rock, geologically synonymous with Eastern Washington, does have commercial uses and buried treasures of its own.

At approximately a dozen sites scattered about the region from Spokane to Goldendale and Pullman to Moses Lake, basalt is quarried by state licensed, commercial operators. Most is used as crushed basalt, the major component in the asphalt that paves the region's highways, driveways, and parking lots. Ken Gibson, superintendent of S&F Construction's basalt mining operation outside Spokane, says the black volcanic rock comprises about 90 percent of asphalt's rock, sand, and oil mixture. He points to its availability, strength and hardness, purity, and 100 percent fracture, which means pieces interlock well providing good packing and little void space, as being ideal for asphalt.

Basalt is a popular landscaping rock and is also used for railbeds and riprap. Some is quarried for building stone and can be seen in countless houses, offices, and municipal buildings throughout the region.

Somehow this rock that looks rather ordinary in natural outcrops makes an extremely attractive black and brown-tone building stone that exudes a sense of permanence and richness when set in mortar. Highway travellers using Snoqualmie Pass, White Pass, Sherman Pass, and sections of other mountain roads in Washington have seen one of the latest uses for crushed basalt along roadsides. Large wire baskets, called gabions, or gabion sections, are designed to keep falling rocks and debris off the highway. They usually are filled with basalt.

At Washington State University a team of scientists led by Dr. R. V. Subramanian has improved a Soviet and Eastern European process for making continuous basalt fibers that look surprisingly like human hair and have a myriad of uses.

Initial research at the Pullman campus began in the early 1970s, funded by grants from the Pacific Northwest Regional Commission, a multi-state organization made up of Washington, Oregon, and Idaho—all states eager to find new economic uses for their limitless supply of the rock. The straightforward procedure begins by electrically heating crushed basalt to temperatures of 1250° to 1350°C. When sufficiently melted, continuous fibers are drawn out through a tiny platinum nozzle on the bottom of a crucible and wound onto a drum. The temperature of the molten basalt and speed of drawing control fiber diameter, roughly the thickness of human hair. Basalt's 10 to 15 percent iron content gives the silky fibers an attractive golden brown color. They are soft to touch and flexible enough to be spun and woven like fiberglass. Thinner, baby-hair fine fibers, dubbed "basalt wool," can be produced with a jet of air.

With strength and flexibility at least as good as fiberglass and a lower raw material cost, basalt fibers may have a promising future as a strengthener for polymers used to make boats, automobiles, recreational equipment and other goods now made with fiberglass. The fibers' resistance to abrasion and corrosion make them suitable for pipe linings. Strength and alkali resistance should make them the first choice of the construction industry which now uses tons of fiberglass and asbestos fibers to reinforce concrete. An especially promising future may lie in their use as an insulation material. Basalt wool not only looks like fiberglass insulation, it has the same insulative, or "R" value.

Not all economic value is tied directly to the volcanic rock; some resources are found between the rocks. Residents are beginning to hear about the potential of thermal waters that underlie their region. Yellowstone National Park's Old Faithful Geyser need not fear any rivals, but the waters pumped from Eastern Washington's basalt field are hot enough to qualify as a low-temperature geothermal resource.

Temperatures, including those of underground water, increase with depth everywhere in the world; in much of Eastern Washington they rise at about twice the expected rate. Geothermal research in the region is in its early stages, but Keith Stoffel, a state geologist based in Spokane, says "things are looking more positive all the time." Over a wide area, wells drawing from a depth of 2,000 feet can yield water temperatures of 85° to 100°F.

Thermal waters so close to the surface suggest an extra-high heat flow from below, perhaps related to the geologic engine responsible for the previous outpouring of

*Opposite: Fresh asphalt on Highway 2 east of Waterville. John Alwin photo*

*Top: Versatile basalt forms the railbed for the Burlington Northern track along the Columbia's north bank near Lyle. John Alwin photo*

*Left: Deep wells like this one going in on the north side of the Rattlesnake Hills tap water hidden in the basalt below. John Alwin photo*

*Above: A WSU process transforms solid and not-so-solid basalt into hair-like fibers and basalt wool.*

basalt. The dense and homogeneous nature of this thick volcanic pile help make it a good conductor of heat, carrying it toward the surface with less loss than with many other rock types. The porous, or vesicular, tops of individual flows, produced when gas bubbles rose toward the surface of the still molten lava, provide zones for subterranean water movement. Geologists can't agree on the importance of joints and faults in water migration. With the basalt of the central Basin being eyed as a nuclear waste repository, some geologists don't like to talk about fractures in deeply buried basalt.

For one rancher outside Ritzville the 95-degree temperature of water from his 2,000-foot-deep well is nothing more than a nuisance. Since it is too hot to be used directly on crops it must be held temporarily in a cooling pond. But increasingly, residents are viewing the underlying thermal waters as an asset, not a liability. The city of Ephrata has taken the lead. Since 1983, 84-degree water from the 1,900-foot-deep municipal well has helped heat the Grant County Courthouse and several Grant County Housing Authority residences. At the city's geothermal heating plant, water temperature is boosted to 120 degrees with electric heat pumps, used for space heating, and then returned to the city drinking-water supply. The innovative pilot project was supported by a federal Housing and Urban Development grant and was the first such closed circuit municipal system in the world. Initial results reduced a $20,000 oil bill to a $2,200 outlay for electricity. There is talk of expanding the system, perhaps to the schools and hospital, but some of the lowest electricity rates in the nation reduce the economic incentive.

Others in Eastern Washington have followed the Ephrata project with great interest and, spurred on by much higher electricity rates, have initiated their own engineering and economic feasibility studies. Fairchild Air Force Base outside Spokane, and the cities of Yakima and Ellensburg are considering tapping low-temperature geothermal energy.

Thermal waters may form the basis for several exotic new industries. Investigators are studying the feasibility of using low-temperature geothermal waters to directly heat large greenhouses for growing tropical house plants, most of which currently are flown into the Pacific Northwest from distant sources. Equally novel is the potential for using the warm waters for aquaculture, perhaps the raising of shrimp. "Othello—Shrimp Capital of the Northwest" and "Ritzville—The Split-leaf Philodendron City" may be Chamber of Commerce slogans of the future.

Sandwiched between basalt flows in the central and western parts of the Basin are markedly different non-volcanic rocks derived from sediments that settled in the bottom of periodic prehistoric lakes. Sandstone and siltstone are the most common, but there are also extensive deposits of diatomite, also known as diatomaceous earth. This white, non-metallic mineral is derived from the intricate, silica skeletal remains of microscopic, single-celled aquatic plants called diatoms. Diatomite deposits up to 35 feet thick suggest the tiny plants flourished in ancient Central Washington.

Eastern Washington's chalk-like diatomite, free of the traces of arsenic that contaminate deposits in some areas, is among the purest in the nation. It has scores of commercial uses, most importantly as an extremely efficient filter aid. Fluids passed through diatomite powder are cleared of suspended solids and even some bacteria. This is especially important in the food processing industry where clarity is important in such fluids as oils, liquid sweeteners, and fruit juices. Diatomite has been used in swimming pool filters for decades, and finds other applications ranging from paint flattening agents and fillers, to pesticide carriers and coating agents.

Eastern Washington's diatomaceous earth has been exploited commercially since the early part of this century. Mines once operated in several locations including outside Ellensburg and in the Royal Slope. Today Witco's two small, open pit mines near George remain as the only operations and, with the new processing plant on the edge of Quincy, provide more than 100 year-round jobs. Production here ranks Witco as the nation's third largest diatomite producer.

The region's most valuable mineral resources may lie buried and undiscovered under its one-to two-mile-thick basalt layer. Basalt does not yield oil or gas, but Shell and ARCO are gambling tens of millions of dollars that oil, or more likely, natural gas, lies trapped in sedimentary rock reservoirs beneath the Basin's thick volcanic sequence. Exploration in the region has been stymied for decades by these overlying rocks since normal seismic exploration techniques could not "see" through the basalt and into potentially oil-and gas-bearing sedimentary formations. The majority of the more than 400 exploratory wells in Washington have been drilled west of the Cascades, most abandoned without even a hint of oil or gas. Today Washington does not have a single producing well. If Shell and ARCO are successful in their multi-million dollar gamble, the state's only commercially productive gas well may be atop a desolate ridge in the Yakima Folds.

The renewal of interest in the oil and gas prospects of Eastern Washington dates from the 1970s. Motivated by the energy crisis, higher oil prices, and more high-tech exploration techniques, companies returned to areas explored decades earlier, ready to look both deeper and more carefully than before. Shell, working jointly with Standard Oil

Company of California, had drilled a well to a depth of 10,655 feet in Benton County in 1958, but had failed to break through the thick layer of basalt. The first peek beneath the basalt came in 1981 in the Yakima Canyon near Roza Dam. At a depth of approximately one mile they punched through the basalt and continued drilling to a state record depth of 16,199 feet. Although both this well and an adjacent much shallower exploration well showed some indications of natural gas, both were plugged and abandoned as dry holes. Total cost—more than $20 million.

Hopes for new-found riches and hub location within a rich oil and gas province were still alive in nearby Ellensburg in 1981 when the company began another well, this one 15 miles east of town on Whiskey Dick Mountain. Like the two Canyon wells, this $10 million, 14,965-foot well produced no significant shows of oil and gas and was abandoned the following year.

Undaunted and armed with new knowledge on the basalt substratum, Shell, this time in conjunction with ARCO, began drilling at yet another location. Selected was a promising site atop the barren crest of the Saddle Mountains, one of the most prominent of the Yakima Folds. The well, 10 miles northwest of Mattawa, was spud on December 20, 1982, projected to reach the 15,000-foot level. Anticlines, geologic structures in which originally flat-lying rock layers are buckled upward, are highly prized by petroleum geologists who frequently find oil and gas trapped in the crests of such folds. The two energy giants were gambling that not only the overlying skin of basalt, but also the underlying sedimentary rocks had been warped upward when the Yakima Folds formed.

As of mid-1984 neither company had disclosed the depth at which the Saddle Mountain well broke through the basalt, but it is assumed to be at about the two-mile

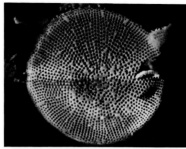

*Above left: Snow-white diatomite at Witco's mine south of George. John Alwin photo     Above right: Delicate diatom skeleton magnified 3,856 times. Richard Pollina photo     Lower right: Veteran Witco mine manager, Harry Ingram, can identify the four grades of diatomaceous earth by feel. John Alwin photo*

level or deeper. In mid-September, 1983, at approximately 12,000 feet, natural gas began flowing up the Saddle Mountain well and ignited an automatic flaring device that lit a 12-foot flame. It burned for days and at night was visible for miles around. The companies dismissed the gas flare as routine, but among many locals it ignited a new wave of optimism about the Basin's natural gas potential. The orange flame made headlines in area newspapers, private pilots flew their planes over the rig to view the spectacle, and so-called "unidentified reliable sources" and "oil industry insiders" suggested this would be a "significant" field.

Two months later, Shell/ARCO announced they would be drilling to a new target depth of 18,000 feet. Drilling at the Saddle Mountain well was completed in March, 1984, at a depth of 17,518 feet, another state record. Comprehensive tests will determine whether this $12 million well is capable of producing enough natural gas to allow commercial production. Both companies and residents in the western part of the Basin eagerly await the results of those tests. Shell already has filed for rights to drill in the nearby Frenchman Hills. Final results at Saddle Mountain will have a bearing on whether Shell continues its Columbia Basin gamble.

# THE PLEISTOCENE EPOCH
## Nature's Grand Finale

Events during the Pleistocene (1.8 million to 10,000 years ago) had a profound impact on Eastern Washington's surface configuration. In many ways this episode constituted the grand finale in shaping much of the natural landscape we know today. The "business as usual" start of the epoch provided no hint of its dramatic and unique finish.

The transition from Pliocene to Pleistocene was imperceptible with processes in the previous epoch continuing into the next. The arching of the Cascades, with an intensification of a rainshadow to the east, the growth of anticlinal folds and downwarping of basins continued without fanfare into the Pleistocene.

At the dawn of the Pleistocene large Lake Lewis (I) innundated the Quincy, Othello, and Pasco basins and adjacent low areas. Geologists can't agree on what obstruction caused the lake to form, but some think the rising Horse Heaven Hills may have acted like a dam, holding back and impounding waters of the Columbia until Wallula Gap was cut and the lake drained. This waterbody and the gravel, sand, silt, and clay deposited by it and the streams that emptied into it may have appeared in the preceding Pliocene. Collectively these sediments, now mostly light-colored, crumbly siltstone and sandstone are called the Ringold Formation. The White Bluffs along the Columbia north of Richland are the Ringold's best-known exposure. Here, the river has cut deeply into the flat-lying 800-foot-thick layer, exposing about 500 feet as scenic white cliffs. Taller than England's famous white cliffs of Dover, the Columbia bluffs are a favorite of passing water recreationists. Fossil bones of vertebrates including those of caribou, camel, ground sloth, peccary, and mastodon unearthed here verify the Pleistocene age of at least the formation's upper section.

The Ringold of the central Basin was a major source for the extensive veneer of wind-blown deposits, or loess, that blankets most of Eastern Washington. This tawny silt unit is called the Palouse Loess, after that corner of the state where it accumulated up to 300 feet thick in places.

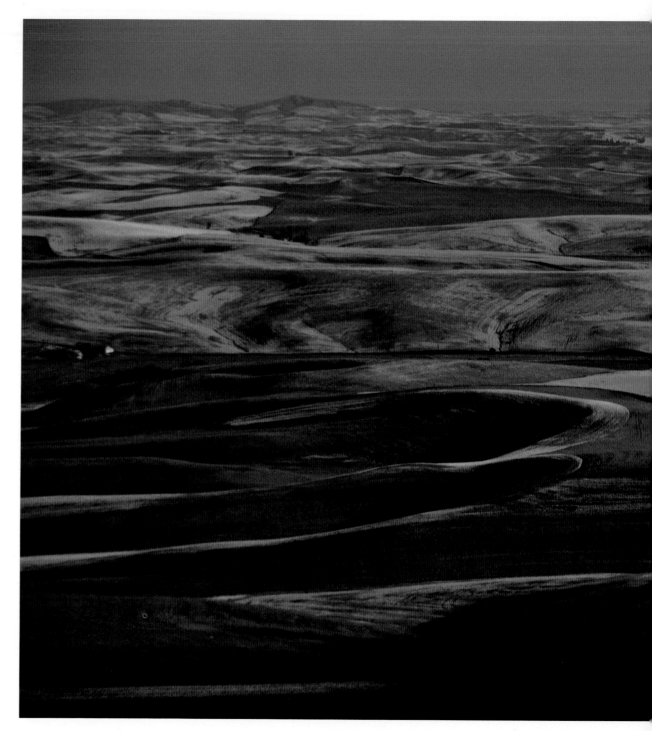

*Above: Ash layers in Eastern Washington document eruptions of Pleistocene volcanoes. More recent was the May 18, 1980 eruption of the Cascade's Mount St. Helens. At Moses Lake a thick layer of the persistent ash still lies at roadside almost a year later. John Alwin photo*

*Left: The sensuous curves of the Palouse Hills are a legacy of Pleistocene and more recent time. View south from Kamiak Butte. John Alwin photo*

Throughout its extent this loessial layer includes large amounts of volcanic ash, evidence of active Pleistocene volcanoes in the Cascades to the west. Within the Palouse, like in much of the region, loess settled directly on basalt surfaces. It is interesting that the upper slopes of steptoes are relatively free of a loess frosting, suggesting they were too steep to permit accumulation of this fine, wind-carried silt.

Even though the pre-loess surface in the Palouse was irregular, it does not explain today's distinctive, rolling Palouse Hills. Physical geographers and geologists have been trying to explain this asymmetrical, wave-like terrain since the 1880s. The sensual curves of these hills are quite varied, but a range of from 100 to 300 feet of local relief and an east-west elongate shape are typical. Steep slopes of 35 percent and more usually are found on northeast sides, while 25 percent and less is more common on southwest-facing slopes. The profile

was once believed to be that of large dunes. Wind action probably was an important factor, but today most researchers agree these unique hills were sculpted from the thick loess layer by a combination of actions. Running water carved a dense network of valleys, stripping away loess, and leaving hills that were further molded and rounded by still other forces. The asymmetry can be explained, in part, by freezing and thawing action under long-lasting snowdrifts on shadier, northeast slopes.

Soils formed on top of loess characteristically are some of the world's most fertile. The extremely rich soils atop the loess on these rolling hills provide the foundation for the phenomenally productive and internationally renowned Palouse wheat region. Loess has continued to be deposited during the last 10,000 years, but unfortunately, destruction of the natural vegetative cover and its replacement by grain and peas over the last century has accelerated the erosion process.

The late Pleistocene is synonymous with the Ice Age, a time when a somewhat cooler, much wetter climate in Canada meant that winter snowfall failed to melt completely each spring. Much remained through the warm season growing deeper each winter. Eventually snow accumulated to great depth in expansive snowfields. When thickness and weight of overlying snow were sufficient, snow at the bottom was transformed to ice, and with continued accumulation began to spread outward under the ponderous snowpack. Eventually two large continental ice sheets thousands of feet thick covered Canada and spilled southward into the United States. The expansive Laurentian Ice Sheet reached to Missouri, but in Washington the Cordilleran Ice Sheet spread only about as far south as the Columbia River.

The first finger-like extensions, or lobes, of the Cordilleran Sheet inched into the large north-south valleys in the Okanogan Highlands, the mountainous area of Washington east of the Cascades and north of the Columbia-Spokane river axis. Here, the lowlands of the Okanogan, Columbia, Colville, and Pend Oreille rivers offered the least resistance to the southward-flowing ice and were eventually filled. As the ice pushed onward it thickened to first hundreds and then thousands of feet, crowding and lapping up mountain sides to bury some intervening highlands.

The most westerly Okanogan lobe was by far the largest in the Okanogan Highlands. At its maximum extent, about 15,000 years ago, it was more than a mile thick at the Canadian border. By then it had pushed 30 miles south of the Columbia onto the Waterville Plateau, the somewhat elevated and levelish northwest corner of the Columbia Basin. An impressive array of textbook examples of glacial landform features remain to document this most ambitious advance of glaciers out onto the basalt field.

Striae and grooves gouged into the basalt by rocks frozen in the overriding base of the ice, and other basalt surfaces polished smooth by the abrasion of sand-laden ice attest to the sliding of the lumbering glacier across this north end of the plateau. Streamlined drumlins formed beneath the advancing ice where movement piled up and molded underlying glacial debris into elongate

J. Harlen Bretz is credited with unraveling the geologic mystery of the Scablands. This 1974 photo taken by his daughter shows Bretz at age 92, six years before his death. A new state park within this unique section of the Northwest seems a fitting memorial to this pioneering geologist. Rhoda Riley photo

ridges shaped like the inverted bowl of a spoon. Drumlins are parallel to the direction of ice movement and have their steepest slopes pointing in the direction from which the ice advanced. On the Waterville Plateau these and other lineal features show that the ice fanned outward once it crossed the Columbia.

The southern limit of the glacier's advance is clearly traced by the Withrow terminal moraine. This is a belt of hilly terrain made up of material the glacier moved like a conveyor belt to its terminus and deposited with the melting ice. The moraine's large size suggests the lobe remained at its terminal position for a long time.

As the ice melted and retreated it left behind still other calling cards. Most apparent are gigantic blocks of basalt called haystack rocks by locals. As the ice pushed onto the plateau it tore up huge blocks of basalt that were picked up and transported southward. When the ice melted these glacial erratics, some larger than a good-size house,

settled to the ground. Now conspicuous sentinels strewn across the landscape, they remain today as mute testimony to the glacier's awesome power.

As striking and varied as they are, the glacial features of the Waterville Plateau are not unique. Similar, and in many cases, even better developed moraines, drumlins, striae, and related features can be seen in other glaciated sections of the United States. Paradoxically, it is farther to the south and east, off the plateau and beyond the reach of Pleistocene glaciers, where the landscape legacy of the Ice Age is of world renown. Not glacial ice, but meltwater from wasting ice in adjacent areas produced one of the most bizarre surfaces anywhere in the world. Here are starkly scenic landscapes stripped clean of overlying loess and soil; deeply scarred with interconnected, steep-walled and dry, rocky coulees gouged into solid basalt; rugged bare-rock buttes and mesas; scoured rock basins; deep piles of gravel and gargantuan ripple marks up to two miles long. The area is appropriately known as the Channeled Scablands. Unraveling the story of its development produced one of the great geologic debates of this century.

Geologist J. Harlen Bretz first studied and named this unique area in the 1920s calling upon a single, short-lived catastrophic flood he named the Spokane Flood, to explain the one-of-a-kind landscape. His hypothesis was considered outrageous and even heretical by many other geologists at the time who rejected his explanation and favored more normal, less cataclysmic processes. Despite the outrage, Bretz persisted, periodically visiting Eastern Washington and publishing on the subject for half a century. His perseverance, eventual corroborative studies by others, and the overwhelming evidence reinforced by satellite images in the 1960s finally convinced the last doubters. His basic hypothesis is now considered scientifically verified.

Scientists still are working out the details and timing of the saga of the Channeled Scablands, but the basic scenario is now fairly well understood. It is a mind-boggling story that cannot be told without liberal use of superlatives. At times it sounds a bit like a tale from Ripley's *Believe It or Not*.

*Upper left: Elephant Rock east of Mansfield, one of many haystack rocks in the region, was dropped by a retreating glacier more than 10,000 years ago. Upper right: In some sections of the Waterville Plateau the gritty bottom of the glacier worked like jeweler's rouge to polish underlying bedrock. Lower right: Streamlined drumlin just south of Mansfield. Lower left: The hummocky Withrow Moraine south of Mansfield traces the southern limit of ice across the Waterville Plateau. John Alwin photos*

Initially, Bretz could not identify a logical source for the huge volume of water responsible for his Spokane Flood. He suggested two possible sources, neither one of which he thought very convincing. One called for a sudden warming of climate with rapid production of meltwater, and the other envisioned volcanic activity beneath nearby glaciers with the resultant great flood.

By the late Twenties Bretz was able to identify the source for at least most of the floodwater in an extensive glacial lake in Western Montana. Field evidence reveals that a lobe of the Cordilleran Ice Sheet pushed far enough south to form a towering ice dam across the Clark Fork River in north Idaho. This 2,000-foot-tall barrier plugged the valley, causing water in the Clark Fork-Flathead drainage to back up and form a giant natural reservoir called Lake Missoula. At its maximum extent the irregular-shaped proglacial lake reached an elevation of 4,200 feet, innundated 2,900 square miles (more than 15 times the area of today's Flathead Lake) and submerged the site of the city of Missoula under 900 feet of water. Faint shorelines of this late-Pleistocene lake remain on the mountain sides above this community and others in Western Montana.

Geologists now know that the ice dam holding back Lake Missoula periodically burst sending as much as 500 cubic miles of water roaring through the Clark Fork Valley toward Eastern Washington, probably exceeding the legal speed limit on today's highways along the route! Calculated peak flow rates of 750 million cubic feet per second (about 15 cubic miles per hour) would have been about 20 times the combined flows of all the world's rivers. Chances are maximum flows lasted only a few hours, with the draining of the lake taking perhaps a week or two.

Even Bretz eventually abandoned the notion of a single flood, but researchers still are trying to decipher the number and timing of the torrents. Modern field studies using radiocarbon dating of organic material trapped in flood deposits and volcanic ash layers of known age suggest there may have been two major episodes of floods, one about 18,000 years ago and the other 13,000 years before the present. Total number of floods may have been in the scores.

The deluges that sent walls of water into the Columbia Basin were the largest yet documented in the terrestrial geologic record. What must have been tidal waves tore into Eastern Washington around the Mount Spokane Highland, pouring into the Spokane area from both the north and east with each bursting of the dam. At the time of at least some of these outbursts the Spokane Valley and a section of the Columbia River downstream were already brimfull with the waters of another Pleistocene lake. Lake Columbia grew behind another ice plug that formed whenever the Okanogan lobe dammed the Columbia River at the north end of Grand Coulee.

The volume of water generated by the floods could not possibly have been handled even by a free-flowing Spokane-Columbia river system. Water poured out to the south, following the natural slope downhill toward the center of the Columbia Basin to the southwest, topographically more than 1,700 feet lower. The fast-moving debacles carried along icebergs, boulders, rocks, gravel, and sand as they charged across the loess-covered lava field. Flood waters did not spread evenly over the Basin, but moved toward the low Pasco Basin through three interconnected southwest routeways.

The 70-mile-long Cheney-Palouse tract is the most easterly and largest of these paths. Its surging torrents, up to hundreds of feet deep, entered the Basin immediately southwest of Spokane along a 20-mile-wide front. Rather than moving down a single large channel, water cut and raced through a series of interlocking channels that frequently overflowed. It ripped through the western edge of the Palouse Hills stripping off overlying loess, some of which was more than 150 feet thick. In places within the tract loess covering remained atop islands that were streamlined by the huge flows and now have a characteristic sharp prow pointing up-current. Larger Palouse Loess "islands" now are farmed and contrast sharply with surrounding barren scabland terrain.

*Faint shorelines of ancient Lake Missoula are still visible on hillsides in western Montana's National Bison Range. John Alwin photo*

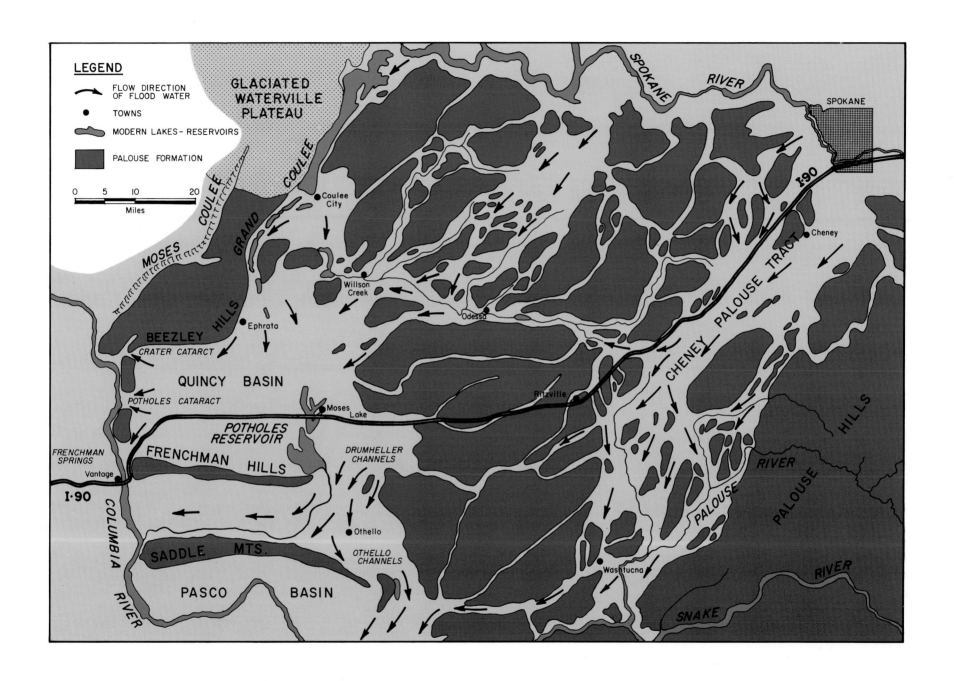

Generalized map of the Channeled Scabland showing direction of flood waters and remnant areas of Palouse loess that survived the debacle. Modified after maps in U.S. Geological Survey, "The Channeled Scablands of Eastern Washington" and H.E. Wright, Jr., Editor, Late-Quaternary Environments of the United States, *Volume 1.*

*Above left: Spring-green Scabland and coulee west of Sprague. John Alwin photo   Above right: Highway 17 north of Soap Lake follows the Grand Coulee's natural corridor. John Alwin photo   Left: Steamboat Rock State Park in upper Grand Coulee. Bureau of Reclamation photo   Below left: Summer Falls, south of Coulee City, once an outlet for flood waters, now directs irrigation water toward the sprawling Columbia Basin Project. Bureau of Reclamation photo*

Erosion didn't stop once the veneer of loess had been stripped away. The erosive power of flood waters was so extreme that basalt bedrock was scoured and deeply gouged. The most impressive scars are the miles-long, steep-sided, rocky trenches known as coulees that were knifed into the bedrock. Flood waters actually quarried, or plucked out, large chunks and peeled off layers of the closely jointed columnar basalt, leaving the giant bare rock chasms that are now usually dry. Potholes, or deep rock basins, huge cataracts, rocky and angular black buttes, and ragged mesas all contribute to these bizarre and wildly scenic scablands.

Still other evidence of the depth and speed of floodwaters is recorded in immense ripple marks with heights of 10 feet and more, some made up of boulder material up to two feet in diameter. In protected areas just down current from obstructions like bedrock projections, a slowing of current caused floodwater to deposit coarse gravel and boulder bars that remain as huge piles.

To the west another ravaging torrent rushed southwestward, entering the Basin between Davenport and Creston along an 18-mile-wide front. Here a similar jumbled, scabland topography stripped free of loess and soil and with a maze of coulees, buttes, mesas, deep rock basins, and giant ripple marks and gravel bars covers an 800-square-mile area north of Odessa. Water passing through this shorter tract flooded into the low Quincy Basin where, for at least awhile, some backed up to form a large lake.

Additional floodwaters entered the Quincy Basin still farther west via the awesome Grand Coulee. Geologists think the route of this largest of Eastern Washington coulees had been cut by the Columbia River prior to the floods, when the southward-pushing Okanogan lobe blocked its previous course and forced the river to cut a temporary detour channel to the east. This most spectacular of the Scabland coulees is about 50 miles long, up to four miles wide, and 900 feet deep. In places it has been cut deeply enough to expose underlying granite rock set in place eons earlier.

# PATTERNED GROUND

## Ice Age Relicts

With the Cordilleran Ice Sheet on the north and mountain glaciers spilling down from both the Rockies on the east and the Cascades to the west, it would be safe to say that Eastern Washington had a super-chilly climate during the last ice age. Extremely cold winter temperatures, wetter conditions than today, and repeated freezing and thawing during the late Pleistocene might explain at least some of the unique patterned ground that covers hundreds, if not thousands of square miles of Washington between the mountains. Geometric shapes range from circles, to polygons, stone nets, and mounds.

As with the more famous Mima Mounds south of Olympia, scientists disagree on what formed these curious features in the loess and loosely consolidated material east of the mountains. Some have called on normal erosion by running water; others suggest they merely reflect the polygonal jointing pattern in the underlying basalt; even industrious ants, fish, and pocket gophers have been credited as the architects of some of the features. But analogy with surface patterns in today's cold-climate areas like Alaska, Greenland, and Siberia, and the probable presence of a near-glacial climate here in the Pleistocene, suggest similar cold-land processes produced Eastern Washington's patterned ground.

Although the mechanisms forming patterned ground are not well understood,

*Low sun of early evening accentuates this patterned ground 15 miles east of Ritzville. John Alwin photo*

intense frost action and freeze-thaw cycles of water-saturated soil are important. Anyone who doubts the power of frost action and its ability to move things about need only talk to farmers. In many sections of the nation where ground freezes during winter, but where climates are far from the glacial end of the scale, farmers must go through their fields each spring picking up rocks that frost heaved onto the surface.

Blister-like mounds anywhere from a few feet up to 100 or more feet in diameter and to seven feet high are Eastern Washington's most ubiquitous type of patterned ground. In places, basalt blocks and fragments, evidently pushed out of the dominantly fine

material in the mound by frost sorting, occur in low areas between mounds producing stone nets and polygon patterns.

Mounds are most abundant in a wide arc beginning in the Horse Heaven Hills on the southwest and extending northward through the Yakima Folds, then eastward through a broad area south of the Columbia River between Wenatchee and Cheney. For travellers on I-90 mounds are most obvious in the Sprague area, especially in the low sun and long shadows of early morning or early evening. These peculiar relics of the Ice Age are most apparent from the air and are well known by Eastern Washington's air travellers.

*Now silent and still, there is an eeriness to the almost four-mile-wide, 400-foot-high Dry Falls. More than twice as high and five times as wide as Niagara Falls, it must have had a roar that echoed for miles every time Spokane Flood waters filled the channel. John Alwin photo*

Grand Coulee's elephantine proportions are the result of erosion during the periodic late-Pleistocene floods that swelled the Columbia to many times its present size and tore through the coulee at speeds up to at least 60 miles per hour. One can best sense the huge volume that must have raced through this channel during peak flood periods at Dry Falls, an almost four-mile-wide and 400-foot-high cliff across the coulee floor. More than twice as high and five times as wide as Niagara Falls, it must have had a roar that echoed for miles every time floodwaters filled the channel. Today the upper coulee has been put to beneficial use holding the waters of Banks Lake, an integral part of the vast Columbia Basin Irrigation Project.

South of Soap Lake, floodwaters from the Grand Coulee fanned out into the Quincy Basin where they combined with flows entering from the northeast and from the Cheney-Palouse tract. Water moving swiftly through the Scablands was able to pick up and carry a huge volume of sand, gravel, and boulders, but lost its transport ability as it backed up in the Quincy Basin. The basin functioned as a vast settling pond, with slack water dropping basaltic sand and gravel to the bottom. These sands and gravels now blanket more than 500 square miles and are up to 180 feet thick.

*Above left: Saucer-shaped Quincy Basin from atop the Frenchman Hills with the Beezley Hills rising in the distance. John Alwin photo*

*Above: Ice-rafted, five-foot-tall granite boulder sits beyond the south end of Lower Grand Coulee, whisked into place by powerful Pleistocene flood currents. John Alwin photo*

*Left: Imaginative lithograph of Grand Coulee from the 1853 Pacific Railroad Survey.*

31

Despite its large size the Quincy Basin was unable to hold all floodwater flowing in and spectacular outlets quickly developed. To the west three great cataracts dumped overflow from the brimfull basin directly into the Columbia River gorge. On the north Crater Cataract was a 200-foot-high waterfall and to the south both Potholes and Frenchman Springs were 400-foot-high, double falls. Potholes was the widest cataract at 1-1/2 miles, but all three left huge gashes especially visible from the air. Highway travellers on Interstate 90 approaching the Vantage Bridge from the east can see where Frenchman Springs waterfall once tumbled over the basalt.

Even more water escaped the Quincy Basin around the lower east nose of the Frenchman Hills anticline where it produced a complex scabland known as the Drumheller Channels. The prodigious discharge through this tract sculpted 100 square miles of some of the most classic scabland to be found anywhere in Eastern Washington. Its labyrinth of deep, rock-walled canyons, buttes, water-eroded pinnacles, basins, and ponds are best viewed looking to the south off the road that crosses O'Sullivan Dam (at the south end of Potholes Reservoir). Once through the channels some water veered west, tearing through the lowland between the Frenchman Hills and Saddle Mountains headed for the Columbia via the Lower Crab Creek drainage. Today, scabland terrain traces that route. Other waters continued southward around the east end of the Saddle Mountains where their erosive power cut the Othello Channels enroute to the Pasco Basin immediately to the south.

All floodwaters converged on the low Pasco Basin and its single outlet through the Horse Heaven Hills at Wallula Gap. Even though water rushed out the mile-wide gap at depths of up to 800 feet, the constriction was too small to accommodate all catastrophic floodwaters. Water backed up into the Pasco Basin and tributary valleys including the Yakima, Walla Walla, and Snake River lowlands forming a temporary lake. Lake Lewis (II) rose to an elevation of 1,150 feet and innundated more than 1,000 square miles at its maximum. For at least a brief period, the site of the Tri-Cities lay submerged under almost 800 feet of water. On the east the site of Walla Walla sat 200 feet under water, and to the west a large arm reached as far up the Yakima Valley as the city of Yakima.

Sand and silt that settled to the bottom of this glacial lake in distinct, rhythmic layers are known as the Touchet Beds. Their buff to cream-colored silt and fine sand layers are a common sight throughout the area of the former lake, especially along Highway 12 west of Walla Walla. The beds commonly include boulders of granite and other non-basalt rocks. The unique nature of some suggest they must have been carried in from as far away as Idaho and northeast Washington, some think locked in large chunks of ice that were carried across the Scablands and set adrift in temporary Lake Lewis. As these icebergs melted, stones and boulders would have fallen to the lake bottom and been covered by silt and sand.

Up to 40 distinct layers have been counted in a 100-foot-thick section of the Touchet Beds in the Walla Walla Valley south of Lowden. Each individual Touchet bed may represent a separate flood (thus 40 floods), each from a different Lake Lewis that may have lasted for only a matter of hours. The span of time between deposition of individual Touchet beds, and thus floods, probably was measured in terms of decades.

Since discovery of the catastrophic outbursts, the term, "Spokane Flood" generally has been replaced with "Missoula Floods." Whatever their names, these largest releases of water ever documented in the earth's history have left an indelible mark on Eastern Washington. It has been estimated that up to 2,800 square miles of the region have been converted into scablands unlike any other place on earth.

*Left: Each rhythmically layered Touchet Bed south of Lowden may represent an individual flood episode. John Alwin photo*

*Below: Flood waters racing through Lower Crab Creek along the north side of Saddle Mountain sculpted bizarre landforms enroute to the Columbia. John Alwin photo*

# WEATHERWISE

Mention the state of Washington in a climatic vein to most people around the nation and they immediately conjure up images of a wet, coolish, and maritime clime. "It rains a lot," they will say. Washingtonians know that more than half the state doesn't conform to that prevalent notion of what is a distinctly west slope regime. East of the blocking Cascades, somewhat removed from the moderating effect of the Pacific Ocean and the moisture it generates, is another Washington with a seasonal clime and annual precipitation totals that classify most of the region as semiarid.

In marked contrast to inland locations where more continental climates prevail, areas near large, unfrozen bodies of water, like the Pacific Ocean or Puget Sound, tend to have relatively moderated and maritime climates. Since these expanses of water both heat and cool more slowly than adjacent land areas, they function to even out temperatures throughout the year. Winters generally don't get extremely cold nor summers oppressively hot. For example, at Seattle the difference between long-term average July and January temperatures equals just 26°F (66° and 40°). East of the mountains the corresponding figure for Spokane is almost double that at 45 degrees (25° and 70°). The plains of Eastern Washington hold the state high-temperature record of a scorching 118 degrees set on July 24, 1928 at Wahluke and again on August 5, 1961 at Ice Harbor Dam on the Snake River. Between January 1937, and December 1968, Deer Park, just north of Spokane, held the record low at minus 42.

Daytime summer temperatures in Eastern Washington are predictably warm to hot. Reliable warm weather and good thermals were the primary reasons for the repeated choice of Ephrata

*Montana already claims title to "Big Sky Country," but Eastern Washington is a prime candidate for the nickname, "Blue Sky Country." John Alwin photo*

Eastern Washington through the seasons . . .

*Above: Fall color along West Sumner on Spokane's South Hill*

*Above right: A Kittitas winter*

*Far right: Wild phlox signals the arrival of spring*

*Right: Wispy fair-weather summer clouds above Moses Coulee, a common sight regionwide during this hot, dry season. John Alwin photos*

as site for such a weather sensitive event as the National Glider Championship. With the 90- to 125-mile-wide and 4,000- to 10,000-foot-high Cascades thwarting the moderating influence of the Pacific, daytime high temperatures in the 90-degree range are common. Average daily temperatures of 70 degrees or more are the norm. The low central Basin focused on the junction of the Snake and Columbia rivers, where elevations fall below 400 feet above sea level, experiences July and August average daily maximums in the low 90s. On at least a few afternoons each summer the mercury climbs over 100. Higher locations on the flanks of the Columbia Basin are spared some of the extreme summer temperatures. Topographically low Kennewick at an elevation of 392 feet has a July average daily maximum of 91.1; whereas the corresponding figure for peripheral Pullman (elevation 2,545) is 81.8; Spokane (elevation 2,349) 84; and Waterville (elevation 2,620) 83.5.

Unlike in the East or Midwest where 90-degree temperatures accompanied by high humidity wilt even the most avid sun worshippers, this is a drier, more bearable heat. The prevailing semiarid clime generally allows temperatures to drop into the comfortable sleeping range of the 50s by night. Once the summer sun sets, the ground radiates heat stored during the day. Because of the low humidity there is little moisture in the air to absorb the heat and re-radiate it back to the land. The same semiarid condition also means night skies free of clouds which would help trap the heat of the day. All bets on the predictability of this natural air conditioning are off during protracted hot spells, when even after sundown temperatures may slip into the 60s on a lucky night, or hover in the 70s, straining air conditioners and ice machines area-wide. These sit-on-the-front-porch nights are most common in the central Basin.

Hot summers go hand-in-hand with sunny skies in Eastern Washington. Percent of possible summer sunshine received averages between 80 and 85 percent. To the delight of farmers and swimming-pool addicts, that figure climbs even higher in such places as Moses Lake, Othello, and the Tri-Cities.

Winters are a time when Pacific weather systems and maritime influence have their maximum effect on Eastern Washington. As the cool season

*This sand dune along the Columbia River could double as a location for a desert scene set in the Sahara. John Alwin photo*

becomes established, counter-clockwise air circulation around an intensifying Aleutian low pressure cell sends unstable airstreams across the Cascades. Pacific air flowing inland is the dominant pattern over the region during winters and explains the relatively mild winter temperatures for inland stations at this latitude. Most all of the region experiences a January average maximum of between 32 and 40, with Richland's 41.1 only slightly less than the 43.9 at Sea-Tac International Airport. Throughout the region front lawns retain some degree of greenness through the winter.

Winter can be cold in Eastern Washington, but ridiculously low temperatures are uncommon. The towering ramparts of the Northern Rockies to the east and the Canadian Rockies farther north usually are sufficient barriers to block the blasts of sub-zero Canadian air masses that spill down into the plains of eastern Montana and North Dakota. Every winter the Montana towns of West Yellowstone and Butte predictably experience overnight lows in the minus 30s and 40s, but that is usually as close as these bone-chilling temperatures get to Eastern Washington.

On an average of once each winter super-chilled air does find its way through the mountain barriers and Eastern Washingtonians experience an unwelcome outbreak of Arctic air. The lowish, north-south trending valleys in the Okanogan Highlands, including the Okanogan, Columbia, and Pend Oreille, are the usual portals by which this frigid southward-moving air is funneled into the Columbia Basin. With some Arctic air invasions these northern valleys are the only sections of the state to experience sub-zero readings. In such cases the mixing of the chilled continental and comparatively mild Pacific air over the valleys warms the air to above-zero readings before it fans out into the Basin.

During more major outbreaks the dominant Arctic air mass can spread a blanket of below-zero readings over much of Eastern Washington. In most years, however, double digit below-zero readings are limited to valleys in the Okanogan Highlands and perhaps only a scattering of stations in the colder, higher, north and east sections of the Columbia Basin. Single digit minus readings are about as chilly as it gets in most of the region during these cold snaps. Residents can recall the recent exceptions in December 1983, the winter of 1978-79, and the record-setting ordeal of December 1968.

A few times each winter residents usually are treated to a hint of forthcoming spring with the arrival of warming chinook winds. Not just any invasion of warmer air is a chinook. A true "snow eater" is limited to gusty, warm westerly winter winds that have just descended the Cascades. Air masses cool and lose moisture as they rise over highlands, but heat up at a more rapid rate on their descent. In Eastern Washington the net effect is an air mass that is both warmer and drier than before it began its ascent on the west side of the mountains. The chinook effect is strongest close to the east foot of the Cascades and weakens in an easterly direction. Well-developed, drying chinook conditions can raise temperatures 20 to 30 degrees or more in a matter of hours and can rapidly melt snowpacks.

# EASTERN WASHINGTON'S NORTH DAKOTA WINTER OF '68-'69

*Periodically, not only does an Eastern Washington winter look like North Dakota's, it feels like one, too. John Alwin photo*

Bad winters are like surgical operations—they increase in severity with each telling. The winter of 1968-69 produced such outrageous weather, the facts are at least as good as fiction. It all began on December 26 when a very unwelcome, deep mass of super-chilled Canadian air began slipping south across the British Columbia-Washington border. Strong northerly and northeasterly winds accompanied this outbreak of extremely cold Arctic air. The northern stations of Chewelah, Republic, Nespelem, and Waterville were among the first to see temperatures plummet to below-zero readings on the 27th. By the following day the cold air blanketed all of Eastern Washington and sub-zero temperatures were common. The mercury continued to fall with the lowest readings occurring on the 30th.

Describing this Arctic air outbreak several months later, ESSA-Weather Bureau State Climatologist, Earl Phillips wrote, "In many respects, this was the most severe outbreak of cold air since the winter of 1949-50." Minimum temperature records were set at numerous stations in both the Columbia Basin and on the east slope of the Cascades. The minus 48°F recorded on December 30 at both Mazama and Winthrop eclipsed the previous state record of minus 42 held since January 1937, by Deer Park, located just north of Spokane. The minus 43 at Chesaw (east of Oroville) also surpassed the previous record. Within Eastern Washington numerous communities set all-time record lows, including La Crosse (–34), Waterville (–33), Colfax (–33), Anatone (–32), Pullman (–32), and Spokane (a more balmy –25).

During the occasional Arctic air outbreaks in Eastern Washington, overnight lows can dip well below zero, but it is rare when the mercury doesn't climb back into positive ground during daylight hours. This Arctic blast proved an unforgettable exception. At Wenatchee, Othello, Quincy, Ellensburg, and several other stations, temperatures did not reach above zero for three or four consecutive days.

The record lows alone would have been sufficient to etch the winter of '68-'69 into Eastern Washingtonian minds; the accompanying heavy snows only served to add insult to injury. Before the Arctic air had retreated, a warmer and more moist air mass from the Pacific crossed the Cascades, riding in atop the colder, heavier underlying air. This triggered heavy snow over a wide area, and was just the first of a series of weather systems that produced snow on most days that January. By the end of the month semiarid Eastern Washington had

snow depths that sounded more like mountain stations—Waterville (45 inches), Davenport (38 inches), Spokane (39 inches), Wenatchee (23 inches), and Goldendale (28 inches), to mention a few. Winds whipped snow into massive drifts isolating many communities. Hundreds of farm buildings were damaged by the heavy snow and several large warehouses in the Spokane area collapsed under its weight.

Then a geology graduate student at Washington State University, I survived the winter of 1968-69. In Pullman the situation was even more extreme than the record books suggest. Even though Pullman's weather station recorded an official low of minus 32 on December 31, that same day the nearby Pullman-Moscow Regional Airport recorded a mind-boggling minus 50 to the U.S. Weather Bureau. Because of the airport station's unofficial status, the minus 50 was not accepted in the Washington record books.

*Ferry Hall parking lot, WSU, December 1968. John Alwin photo*

Most students were off campus on Christmas break when the low temperatures and deep snows (including a record 24-hour snowfall) struck. Unfortunately this meant living quarters were left empty with thermostats set low. Greek Row suffered heavy damage as one heating system after another froze causing radiators to burst, sending water onto walls and floors. Fourteen Greek houses reported serious damage. Elsewhere on campus bursting water pipes caused thousands of dollars damage in married student housing.

I had never experienced such cold temperatures, deep snows, or worse drifting. My room in old Ferry Hall was poorly heated. My prized, 1951 Ford pickup truck wouldn't start and walking downtown to Charlie Brown's was out of the question. When my daughter is old enough to understand, she will hear the saga of Eastern Washington's North Dakota winter, no doubt complete with appropriate embellishments.

*Top: Test turbines harness the persistent winds on the Goodnoe Hills outside Goldendale. John Alwin photo*

*Bottom: West of Wilbur. Pioneer farmers were quick to discover the potential of Eastern Washington's wind power. John Alwin photo*

The general dryness of Eastern Washington is linked to the rainshadow effect of the Cascades. As Pacific air masses rise over the range, air is cooled and its capacity to retain moisture reduced. Much of the moisture precipitates out on the westward, or windward, side and in summit areas. Most crest locations get more than 80 inches of precipitation per year, with the wettest section of the North Cascades receiving more than 120 inches in an average year. Such mountain-induced moisture is called orographic precipitation. Once over the Cascade barrier the subsiding air warms as it flows down the east slope. Since warming air can hold progressively more moisture it is less likely to release precipitation. Situated on the lee side of the Cascades, Eastern Washington has a classic rainshadow location.

Even though residents refer to large sections of Eastern Washington as desert, most of the region is more correctly classified as semiarid, or steppe, one wetness class above arid (desert). True climatic desert lands are surprisingly restricted in size and limited to sections of the lower Yakima Valley, lands close to the confluence of the Snake and Columbia rivers, parts of the U.S. Department of Energy Hanford Project area, and a narrow belt up the Columbia River to just north of Vantage. Even those driest sections barely qualify as desert. Long-term climatic data show some Yakima Valley stations, including Wapato and Sunnyside, are desert, but not modestly "wetter" Yakima or Moxee. Richland and Kennewick are classed as desert, but just slightly higher average precipitation and cooler temperatures mean Othello and Moses Lake are steppe. Desert conditions in these areas probably cover little more than 1,000 square miles. True desert is so restricted in Eastern Washington that it usually is not differentiated on world or even national climate maps.

_The low central Basin forms the center of a distorted bull's eye pattern on a map of Washington's Average Annual Precipitation._

_Modified after WSU Extension Bulletin 703_

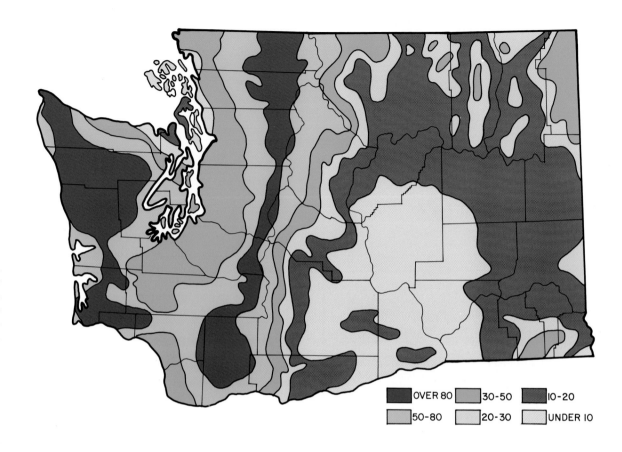

| | OVER 80 | | 30-50 | | 10-20 |
| | 50-80 | | 20-30 | | UNDER 10 |

Within the region terrain and elevation explain the overall pattern of average annual precipitation. As air descends the east slope of the Cascades there is a dramatic drop in precipitation with decreasing elevation. Snoqualmie Pass high in the Cascades at 3,020 feet averages 108 inches of precipitation per year. At Cle Elum, only 29 miles southeast but at an elevation of 1,920 feet, the corresponding figure decreases to 22.6 inches. At the Ellensburg airport (elevation 1,727), 21 miles farther southeast, precipitation averages 8.8 inches annually. East of Ellensburg the precipitation declines less rapidly to 6-1/2 inches 30 miles away at Vantage (elevation 500) on the Columbia River. Descending air and low elevations help explain similar low annual precipitation in the Yakima Valley and Eastern Washington's arid heart near the confluence of the Snake and Columbia.

Conversely, east of the topographically low Columbia River axis precipitation increases with elevation up the east flank of the Columbia Basin. Over the 140 miles between Vantage and the Washington-Idaho border, elevation rises from approximately 500 to 2,600 feet. Continuing the west-east transect up the east flank of the Basin, elevation, orographic lifting, and corresponding precipitation totals increase far less dramatically than on the Basin's much steeper west slope. Thirty-seven miles east of Vantage at Moses Lake (elevation 1,208) average annual precipitation increases to just 7.7 inches, at Ritzville (elevation 1,830) 43 miles farther up-slope, the figure rises only slightly to 11.3 inches, but climbs to 21.3 inches 63 miles away near Pullman (elevation 2,545). When viewed on a general scale the Columbia Basin precipitation pattern approximates a partial bull's eye with the driest areas at the center and progressively higher precipitation in each successive outer ring.

The Columbia Basin is far from a smooth-surface bowl; local and regional topographic features distort a perfect bull's eye precipitation pattern. High areas that reach even a few hundred feet above surrounding terrain can trigger localized orographic precipitation. Such elevated tracts as the Saddle Mountains, Rattlesnake Hills, and Horse Heaven Hills receive up to several inches more than adjacent lowlands. In the Palouse islandish steptoes stick far enough above the rolling grass-and-grain mantled landscape to pick up higher precipitation totals. On Kamiak Butte moisture supply is sufficient to support a forest. Even these relatively low "highlands" can create their own rainshadows. Off the northeast, rainshadow end of the Rattlesnake Hills in the Hanford Project, an extra-dry 150 square miles south of Highway 24 and west of Highway 240 have been set aside as an Arid Lands Ecology Reserve. Farmers are most aware of local orographic influence and know where precipitation totals are extra-high or low within their districts.

Consistent with most of the Pacific Northwest, Eastern Washington receives the majority of its moisture during winter, between 65 and 70 percent of annual precipitation in the six-month period

*North foot of Manastash Ridge. The cool temperatures of the fall harvest season mean frequent morning fog in sections of the Kittitas Valley. John Alwin photo*

of October through March. Summer rain is especially sparse, with stations including Yakima, Wapato, Sunnyside, Richland, Othello, Moses Lake, and Wenatchee receiving less than one-quarter inch of rain in an average July! A contraction of the Aleutian low and strengthening of a high pressure cell in the northern Pacific in spring and summer generate a prevailing westerly and northwesterly flow. This air is comparatively dry and cool, and warms as it moves overland. The farther it moves inland the warmer, drier, and more stable it becomes—conditions that are unlikely to produce much moisture. During July and

August, it is not uncommon for four to six weeks to pass without measurable rainfall in the driest areas. In 1925 Yakima went 88 consecutive days without rain. Such dry growing seasons mean that irrigation is essential for farming in many sections.

During winter the Aleutian low generates westerly and southwesterly winds over the Basin. The moist, unstable air comes right off the ocean with a temperature near that of the water. As it moves inland across the cooler land, precipitation is triggered. Even after dumping an average of 400 inches of snow each winter on higher sections of

the Cascades (1,000 inches at Mt. Rainier-Paradise Ranger Station in 1955-56), enough moisture remains to give Eastern Washington its "wet" season.

In the coldest months, heat is lost overnight by radiation. Moist air coming across the Cascades mixes with the colder air in this inland basin, resulting in fog, cloudiness, and occasional ice storms, known locally as silver thaws. The biggest wonder of all is that during winter there is slightly more sunshine in coastal Washington than in Eastern Washington. Wintertime relative humidity in the 70 to 80 percent range is standard, and percent of possible sunshine received falls to 20 to 30 percent—both sharp contrasts to the dry, sunny summers.

41

# VEGETATIVE MOSAIC

If Western Washington is shades of emerald, moss, and deep forest green, then Eastern Washington is a more dusty sage green, with only seasonal splashes of the verdant tones so prevalent in the well-watered west. Sunny shades of sand, buff, and basaltic brown predominate on this leeward side of the mountains.

Eastern Washington lies at the northern appendage of a vast intermontane dryland that stretches from deep within Mexico northward into British Columbia's southern interior. Situated in the rainshadow of high blocking mountain ranges to the west, most of this extensive territory is too dry for the natural growth of trees. Sagebrush provides the dominant ground cover over much of this section of the western United States. Only in the driest quarters are there true desert plant communities. These are most extensive in the south, where they include infamous Death Valley, the Mojave, and the distinctive saguaro cactus deserts of southern Arizona. Farther north, desert tracts appear as smaller, islandish pockets within the engulfing sagebrush zone. Only on the wettest margins does sage yield its dominance to grasses.

Members of the historic Lewis and Clark Expedition were the first non-Indians to visit the Washington section of this expansive dryland. The treeless country was a welcome sight when viewed from afar by members of the Corps of Discovery as they descended the west slope of the Rockies in September 1805. After days of snow, cold, difficult mountain terrain, depleted provisions, and a dearth of wild game, the mere sight of the "Prairie country," as Captain Lewis called it, was a "cheering prospect" and cause for "inexpressable joy."

*Eastern Washington is a dusty sage green, with only seasonal splashes of the verdant tones so prevalent in the well-watered west. John Alwin photo*

*Just east of Pasco. It is peaceful, late summer scenes like this that make former Eastern Washington residents home-sick. John Alwin photo*

With winter approaching as they closed in on their Pacific objective, the trail weary explorers assumed the more open, less rugged country and its navigable rivers would mean greater speed and ease of travel. If like other plains areas they had traversed, the open country could be expected to provide an abundance of big-game animals to re-stock their depleted food supply.

Reaching the Clearwater River in northern Idaho, the footsore party gratefully took to canoes, floating down that tributary and into the Snake River, entering Washington at today's Clarkston. Unfortunately the explorers skirted only the south-ern edge of the Columbia Basin. Drifting down the Snake, these first white explorers of record saw little of the country from the bottom of this 2,000-foot-deep canyon. Not until they reached the Pasco Basin did the deeply incised river break out onto a plain and the true nature of the adjacent country become apparent.

Describing the land near the mouth of the Snake, Captain Lewis wrote, "There is on this plain no tree, and scarcely any shrubs, except a few willow-bushes; even of smaller plants there is not much more than the prickly-pear [cactus], which is in great abundance, and is even more thorny and troublesome than any we have yet seen." This observation was made in one of *the* driest sections of Eastern Washington, but others made along the Snake and farther downriver on the Columbia reinforced the less-than-positive environmental image of the Columbia intermon-tane region as a levelish, dry, largely treeless area with a sparcity of game.

The initial desolate image was changed only marginally when the Expedition re-crossed the southern fringe on their 1806 return home. Travel-ling up the Columbia that spring, Captain Lewis scaled the canyon wall in the vicinity of modern McNary Dam and saw level plains spreading out to the horizon. They were covered with an abun-dance of low grass that he assumed to be "unusu-ally nutritious" based on the plumpness of horses that had wintered over on this dry bunch grass. At the mouth of the Walla Walla River the entou-rage left the Columbia and struck out overland along an Indian trail that crossed the "high

Above: This vista of flat-topped, broken terrain southeast of Day-ton, minus the golden grain fields, greeted Lewis and Clark on their legendary 1806 return from the Pacific. John Alwin photo

Left: The awesome chasm of the Tucannon River Valley north of the Blue Mountains presents almost as much challenge to trav-ellers on Highway 126 as it did to Lewis and Clark more than 170 years ago. John Alwin photo

plains" between the Snake River and Blue Moun-tains, passing by the sites of Waitsburg, Dayton, and Pomeroy.

Initial observations along this section con-firmed the desolation. The journal records they entered "an open, level, sandy plain, unbroken except by large banks of pure sand, which have drifted in many parts of the plain to the height of 15 or 20 feet." But farther east on the topographic-ally higher and less dry northern flank of the Blue Mountains the country improved. Trees, and thus firewood, became more abundant, streams were more numerous, rich loam soil supported taller, knee-high grasses and fewer "aromatic shrubs" (sagebrush), and game once again became plenti-ful. Clearly this was a very different environment, one which Captain Lewis compared to the "plains on the Missouri" minus the vast herds of buffalo, elk, and other game animals. It was described as a "beautiful fertile and picturesque country" and there was no doubt that "if cultivated would pro-duce in great abundance."

Based on the limited traverse by Lewis and Clark, it was apparent that the treeless Columbia Basin was not everywhere the same, an observation lost on some subsequent visitors. Had the Expedition the charge to explore Washington's entire intermontane region in the years before white occupance, this diversity would have been even more obvious.

Prior to the arrival of domesticated livestock, natural vegetation within the Basin had adjusted

ton northward-extending stringers carry this zone outside the Basin up both the Methow and Okanogan valleys, the latter connecting with the sagebrush country of interior British Columbia.

In the driest sections, bunch grass is short and appears only as scattered tufts interspersed between and below a sagebrush overstory. On topographically higher and marginally wetter areas like the Yakima Folds and the gentle east slope of the Columbia River, the perennial grasses are

to local and regional variations in climate, soil, elevation, and slope. The natural vegetation of most of the tract is classified as steppe, or grassland. In moist grasslands, or true prairies, grass cover is carpet-like, but here a more discontinuous bunch grass is the most widespread cover. Blue bunch wheatgrass is the dominant species. Both it and its admixture of plants vary markedly over the region and constitute much of the basis for the region's major non-forested vegetation zones.

North and west of an imaginary line running between Pasco and Spokane, a dominantly sagebrush and bunch grass plant community prevails. This driest 70 percent of the Basin is classic steppe, the most widespread vegetative zone in the three Pacific Northwest states. Within Washing-

more robust. The greater abundance of these nutritious grasses atop the largest of the Folds once provided excellent range for horses earning it the name, Horse Heaven Hills.

With its scorching summer temperatures, distant vistas distorted by heat waves, days stretching into weeks without as much as a drizzle, tumbleweed, rattlesnakes, horned lizards, even scorpions and sand dunes, it is no wonder residents refer to much of this sagebrush country as "the desert." Botanists would agree that many tracts do have desert characteristics but probably would reject a desert label on technical grounds. The presence of grasses in even the driest quarters rules out classification as true desert based on vegetation alone.

*Left: Sparse vegetation in the Black Sands area north of Royal City. John Alwin photo*

*Above: Aptly named and ubiquitous bunch grass. Joel W. Rogers photo*

*Left: Eastern Washington vegetation at its photographic best. Early fall in the Yakima Canyon. Top: Highway 221 north out of Patterson snakes across the sage and grain fields of the Horse Heaven Hills toward Prosser. Bottom: Animal tracks record earlier passage of wildlife over the snowy, sage-covered plains of the central Basin. John Alwin photos*

# SAGEBRUSH

Most residents of Central Washington's shrub-steppe can't identify Blue bunch wheatgrass, but they all know sagebrush on sight. Following occasional summer rains the distinctive scent of this aromatic shrub fills the air, reminding even city dwellers that they live in sagebrush country. Perhaps no other plant so represents the Old West than this abundant shrub of the sunflower family. Nevada has claimed the sagebrush as its state flower; Central Washingtonians will have to settle for an unofficial, "regional flower" status.

Sagebrush probably spread into Washington from older, established dry areas to the south when the rising Cascades intercepted enough moisture to produce a semiarid climate east of the mountains. Sage is one of the few woody plants that has adapted to life in the semiarid steppe. This drought resistant plant has developed characteristics that permit it to survive Central Washington's hot and dry summers.

Critical to survival is the absorption of as much precious water as possible and its retention during summer. To maximize water absorption, sagebrush has a well-developed root system. Deep tap roots reach down ten feet or more in search of moisture. Closer to the surface smaller, wide-spreading roots take advantage of moisture from light rain, absorbing water before it evaporates. Leaves, which are retained year-round, are small, with little surface area through which moisture can be lost by transpiration. Leaf surfaces are covered with fine hairs which further limit transpiration by reflecting sunlight and buffering the inevitable desiccating winds. Conservation of moisture is also enhanced as sagebrush becomes somewhat dormant during the driest parts of the year. In Central Washington these plants

*Sage-accented landscape in the Lower Grand Coulee east of Lake Lenore. John Alwin photo*

are more active in January than in the heat of midsummer. Sagebrush experiences its maximum growth during late winter and spring, and does not bloom with its numerous, tiny yellow flowers until late summer or early fall.

Sagebrush will not thrive, as is commonly believed, in just any dry area. It is surprisingly sensitive to moisture and soil conditions. It does best in deep and relatively moist, sandy soils where the Big Sagebrush species so common in this region can reach heights of six feet. In drier, stonier, and poorer soil areas sagebrush size and robustness decline.

East of the imaginary Pasco-to-Spokane line, shrub-steppe yields to true steppe. Increasing annual precipitation and somewhat cooler temperatures limit sagebrush and allow bunch grasses to thrive. On the higher, wetter eastern fringe the Columbia Basin's virgin vegetative mantle historically was at its most luxuriant. In a small area on the northern and western flanks of the Blue Mountains and within a 30-mile-wide swath of territory hugging the state line and extending northward to just outside Spokane, natural grasses were especially lush and stood at least stirrup-high when the first whites arrived. In this Palouse Prairie, grass cover was dense enough to form a turf, or sod-like cover, unlike the sparser covering in the the majority of the Basin to the west. The term, Palouse, is thought to have originated from the French word *pelouse,* meaning lawn or greensward, and to have been applied to this region by early Jesuit missionaries. Under this more subhumid climate, a large number of forbs like balsamroot, lupine, and geranium, as well as bushes, including snowberry and wild rose, added to the prolific vegetative mantle. Over millenia this rich grass covering added organic matter and nutrients to the Palouse soil, contributing to the foundation for one of the world's premier dryland grain farming districts.

The rise of the Cascade Range in the Pliocene-Pleistocene led to the gradual drying of climate and the decline of once extensive Columbia Basin forests. Today forested areas are the exception within this dominantly treeless, grass and sagebrush region. In most quarters sinuous riverside stands of cottonwood and willow are the only "forests" for miles in all directions. Only on the Basin's higher and wetter rim areas are trees more common, and rarely do they reach very far onto the basalt plains.

Most common are the Basin's encircling ponderosa pine forests. This largest of Washington's needled pines, with its distinctive elephant-hide bark, is readily recognizable and is probably known by more local names (yellow pine, bull pine, blackjack pine) than any other state tree. Drought resistance explains the presence of *Pinus ponderosa* in Eastern Washington. The tree cannot compete with other conifers like Douglas fir in wetter environs, but it easily dominates in the dry

forest margins where summer drought rules out other species except in a few scattered and atypical sites.

Ponderosa pine constitutes the lowest forest zone on the eastern flank of the Cascades and extends into our Eastern Washington region on higher tracts including the Simcoe and Wenatchee mountains, Umtanum and Manastash ridges, and sections of the Yakima Indian Reservation. On the southeast, this long-needle pine dominates the grassland-to-forest transition zone around the flank of the Blue Mountains. To the north, it spills over onto the south side of the Columbia and Spokane rivers where the tree is abundant in the rugged breaks country. Metropolitan Spokane is largely "in the trees" and a 200-square-mile prong of ponderosa carries the forest almost 30 miles farther onto the basalt plain. Travellers heading west out of Spokane via I-90 don't break out of the trees until about 25 miles southwest of the city, and those driving toward Pullman on well-travelled Highway 195 don't see the southern edge of the pines in their rear-view mirror until approaching Spangle. Cheney, Medicine Lake, and several other communities are tucked away in this picturesque pine-clad country.

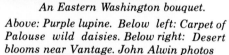

*An Eastern Washington bouquet.*
*Above: Purple lupine. Below left: Carpet of Palouse wild daisies. Below right: Desert blooms near Vantage. John Alwin photos*

48

*Balsamroot among the ponderosa south of Cheney.*
*John Alwin photo*

This most ambitious incursion of trees out onto the plain southwest of Spokane can be partly explained by the area's slightly higher precipitation and cooler climate. Lower summer temperatures here mean less precipitation is lost to evaporation and more is available for tree growth. The inability of shallow-rooted young seedlings to live through summer drought appears to be a limiting factor in the expansion of this forest.

Most other tree-covered areas owe their existence to localized precipitation or slope orientation. Higher steptoes and some hills near Spokane trigger enough orographic precipitation to support tree cover. On Kamiak Butte north of Pullman conditions are wet enough for stands of moisture-loving western red cedar and western larch, in addition to Douglas fir on the cooler and shadier north slope. In the Palouse River Valley at Colfax and along other protected river valleys within the Palouse, especially on north-facing slopes, ponderosa pine and even some Douglas fir thrive and provide a pine-scented setting for residents of this dominantly treeless country.

When the first whites of record arrived in Eastern Washington almost 200 years ago, they found a vegetative mosaic that had been only marginally impacted by people and animals. Unlike farther east in the Great Plains where millions of buffalo grazed and trampled the grassland, and where native inhabitants greatly altered the vegetative component by repeated burning, these major elements of change largely were absent in most of the Columbia Basin.

Following glacial times bison were never numerous in the region and were few in number, then non-existent over the last 2,500 years. Even at the time of Lewis and Clark's visit, antelope were not plentiful and deer clung closely to the Basin's forested margins. Since it had not been subjected to large herds of native ungulates, the steppe of Eastern Washington had not adapted to heavy grazing pressure.

Even the arrival of horses among the region's natives in the first half of the 1700s probably had minimal impact on natural vegetation.

Within much of the steppe, game was scarce and perennial streams were few and far between. Indians congregated along major rivers where they depended on salmon as their staple. This clustering in river valleys, preferably adjacent to more game-rich forested highlands, held villages to the periphery, leaving much of the Basin void of permanent residents. According to Dr. Rexford Daubenmire, noted international botanist and former professor of Botany at Washington State University, overgrazing and vegetation damage by Indian horses probably was restricted to areas adjacent to riverside villages. Daubenmire also has suggested that aboriginal use of fire was quite limited since there were few big-game animals to be harvested with its use, and fire as a weapon in warfare made little sense when villages were so close to rivers.

Large-scale modifications of Eastern Washington's vegetative mosaic did not begin until the arrival of whites and their animals during the nineteenth century. Over a span of less than a century, overgrazing by livestock, plowing up of natural vegetation to make way for dryland grain crops, wholesale invasion by alien weeds, range improvement programs, and conversion of still more shrub-steppe into irrigated fields have greatly reduced areas of virgin and near-virgin vegetation. Today relict areas are limited to small patches in protected or remote sites. Fenced pioneer cemeteries in rural areas and drier tracts far removed from water, beyond the range of intensive grazing, account for most of these vegetative vestiges.

Initial impact on vegetation was minimal as was the number of both livestock and settlers. The first sizable herd of cattle to arrive in Eastern Washington was the more than 600 head driven to the Whitman Mission, near Walla Walla, from California in the 1830s. Distance from markets and Indian wars between 1845 and 1855 kept cattle numbers low, but by the late 1850s and early 1860s the situation had changed dramatically. By then military posts like Fort Dalles, Fort Simcoe, Fort Walla Walla, and Fort Taylor, and now fa-mous battles including those at Steptoe, Spokane Plains, and Four Lakes had, in the parlance of the time, secured the frontier. Almost simultaneously discovery of rich placer gold deposits nearby provided a new regional market for meat. In quick succession colors were struck to the north in British territory in the Cariboo, Fraser, and Kootenai districts, to the east in what soon became western Montana, in today's Idaho at the Clearwater, Salmon, and Boise diggings, and to the south at John Day. There was even a revival of interest in Washington's own Colville mines. With such lucrative markets a large-scale range cattle industry began in earnest on Eastern Washington's steppe lands.

Livestock interests discovered that cattle thrived on the region's virgin bunch grass, just as Lewis and Clark had suspected a half-century earlier. Commenting on the forage quality of these grasses, Lieutenant Thomas W. Symons, the leader of a later 1881 federal government survey of the Basin wrote, "I have been told by an old pioneer packer, who for many years packed through the country, that his animals would keep in better condition on bunch-grass alone than they would if fed on ordinary hay and grain. 'Bunch-grass' has become the synonym for things good, strong, rich, and great; the bunch-grass country is the best and finest country on earth, bunch-grass cattle and horses are the sweetest, fleetest, and strongest in the world . . ."

Cattle herds flooded in. Once fattened on the unfenced free range they were driven via the Cariboo, Colville, Mullen, and other soon well-worn trails and roads to the meat-hungry miners. It was a lucrative business that took its toll on Eastern Washington's natural vegetation. The native range already showed signs of deterioration by the late 1860s. Once the gold flush was off and boom turned to bust, demand for meat dried up. By the 1870s cattlemen were without markets and range was severely overstocked.

Overgrazing reduces the density of large, more nutritious and desirable perennial grasses like Blue bunch wheatgrass and Idaho fescue. These were especially sought by cattlemen in the spring when the tall grasses were soft and a favorite of cattle. The herds could fill up and gain weight more quickly on taller grasses, known as "ice cream plants" by those in the trade. But as these early-growing, late-maturing grasses were grazed closely, seed formation was lost and nutrients could not be stored in roots. Many plants died and those that remained were weakened, unable to

*Tree-crested Kamiak Butte from the south. John Alwin photo*

*Right: Grazing range cattle dramatically altered Eastern Washington's natural vegetation. Eastern Washington Historical Society photo  Far right: Ponderosa parkland in the Turnbull National Wildlife Refuge south of Cheney. John Alwin photo Below: Placid Lake Blackmore, in the Turnbull, is prime waterfowl habitat. John Alwin photo*

compete against the less desirables, like sagebrush in drier areas, that moved in to occupy the relinquished space. Preferred grasses were crowded out and in places were replaced by injurious and poisonous plants. In short order the "ice cream" plants yielded to less desirable "hardtack."

Eastern Washington's range cattle industry reached its zenith in the 1870s and faded the next decade, replaced by smaller-scale ranching. Devastating winters, the lure of more promising range in the northern Great Plains, and barbed wire fences of a steadily increasing army of farmers contributed to its demise. Even after its death the legacy of the range cattle industry continued to take its toll on the region's vegetation. Innumerable horses previously employed in the industry were set free to become the nucleus of the feral herds. They contributed to overgrazing in some sections and remained a problem until most were captured just after the turn of the century and shipped out of state. As cattle numbers dwindled, sheep flocks

51

# CHEATGRASS

With the first Eastern Washington agriculturists and their crops came the weeds that are still the scourge of farmers and ranchers. Most ubiquitous is infamous cheatgrass (*Bromus tectorum*), a winter annual that probably originated in the Mediterranean Basin. It is the most aggressive of the alien imports and thrives under the region's Mediterranean-like annual precipitation cycle with a summer drought and winter concentration of moisture. This weed with its bowed head can be seen almost everywhere, growing out of sand dunes, along roads and railroad tracks, in fields, and even as the dominant species in some range.

Evidence strongly suggests that cheatgrass entered the Columbia Basin as a grain contaminant, perhaps in adulterated seed grain supplied by less-than-honest dealers. Its presence in the Pullman area may be linked to the college experimental farm where, paradoxically, seed was sown and tested in 1897 as a promising new grass for Eastern Washington's deteriorated range. It began appearing in grain-growing districts in the 1890s, living up to its name by "cheating" grain farmers of yields. Its range quickly expanded outward from these initial centers along connecting rail lines, finding ideal environments in the region's overgrazed range and freshly plowed winter wheat fields. Some of the earliest occurrences were along the trampled cattle trails that previously had led herds to the mining districts during the gold rush era. By the late 1920s cheat already had reached its present distribution and achieved status as one of Washington's most widespread plants.

*Breaking virgin prairie the hard way. Eastern Washington Historical Society photo*

increased. In many areas sheep picked up where cattle left off on the already overgrazed land, leaving many sections in a "sheeped off" condition. Combined, the grazing pressure of cattle, feral horses, and sheep did more to modify Eastern Washington's vegetative mosaic in a few decades than nature had in preceding centuries. And the changes had only begun!

By the 1880s Eastern Washington was firmly in the grip of an agrarian invasion that would impact vegetation even more than livestock overgrazing. Farmers had discovered the grain-growing potential of the loess-derived soils in a broad arc from the Walla Walla country to the Palouse and into the Big Bend area. Railroads served several districts and more were projected to help transport the region's bounty to distant markets. Cropping districts expanded, and between the 1880s and World War I millions of acres of steppe and shrub-steppe were lost. Much of what once had been bunch grass prairie was swiftly and dramatically converted into golden grain fields. Spurred on by the hype of land promoters, wet years, and high prices, these hopeful dryland farmers invaded even the ill-suited, near-desert sections of the central Basin. Transforming the grassland into an agrarian landscape, farmers in-advertently introduced alien weed species which persist today, especially ubiquitous cheatgrass.

Range improvement programs, often synonymous with elimination of sagebrush, have further modified sections of Eastern Washington's shrub-steppe. Within this vegetative zone, large-scale expansion of 20th century irrigated farming has converted more than one-and-a-half million acres of mostly sagebrush steppe into farmland.

Over the last 120 years people and their animals have profoundly altered Eastern Washington's vegetative mosaic. In the process of making this one of the nation's most productive farming districts, almost all natural vegetation has been lost. Even in the most remote, non-farming districts, the vegetation that grows today is probably markedly different from what Lewis and Clark would have seen.

No one would suggest the area be returned to nature and the agricultural cornerstone of the region's economy abandoned. But an increasing number of environmentally aware Washington residents want to see some of the few remaining remnants of virgin vegetation and associated ecosystems protected to assure the preservation of these living museums of the state's natural heritage.

*The geometry of agrarian occupancy in the southern section of the Columbia Basin Project. U.S. Bureau of Reclamation photo*

*Oak groves west of Wishram near their northern limit in the Pacific Northwest. John Alwin photo*

# HOLDING ON
# TO WHAT REMAINS

When people move into an unsettled area they invariably set about modifying the land, converting previously natural landscapes to cultural landscapes. After generations of occupance, humanity's signature on Eastern Washington is everywhere, from its cities, towns, and hamlets, to agricultural fields, dams, reservoirs, and highways, right down to the less obtrusive, yet well-developed complement of introduced weeds. The pattern or imprint of people's environmental modification is best viewed from above, where the geometric patterns and straight lines preferred by *Homo sapiens sapiens* contrast with nature's own design.

Within Washington and the entire Pacific Northwest, an increasingly environmentally aware public, spurred by growing population and land use pressures and the spectre of an entirely cultural landscape, has been striving for protection of at least some of the remaining natural areas. Largely unaltered ecosystems along with their community of plants, animals, and associated features are recognized as irreplaceable elements in the region's rich natural heritage and diversity. Once identified and protected these ecologically significant tracts serve as living museums and outdoor laboratories for educational and research purposes. Some provide critical habitat for endangered or rare plants and animals. All give society a base line, or yardstick, against which past, present, and future human environmental alterations can be measured.

Some preservation efforts meet with a great deal of opposition, especially when they involve relatively large parcels. The battles between pro- and anti-development camps over wilderness designation in Washington's mountainous regions are notorious for their high decible levels. Strange as it may sound, emotions have run just as high over a shrub-steppe, semi-desert area proposed for designation as the Columbia Basin's first federal wilderness area. Some think a wilderness in a desert wasteland makes no sense—who ever heard of a wilderness area without mountains and "real" forests, they ask.

The Juniper Forest, 13 miles northeast of Pasco, recently has been the center of an emotionally charged exchange no less intense than those over pristine sections of the high Cascades. Stands of western juniper within an active sand dune field make this 19,000-acre tract unique within Eastern Washington. Its six groves and scattered individuals around the periphery comprise intermontane Washington's largest stand of western juniper, and constitute the approximate northern limit of the species' range in North America. This unique ecosystem provides important habitat for 10 of the state's 20 to 25 breeding pairs of ferruginous hawk, Washington's only scaled quail population, and other rare animals, including the distinctive Ord's kangaroo rat and diminutive pygmy rabbit.

For years Washington's environmental community has lobbied for federal wilderness designation as the best means of protection for the Juniper Forest's 8,500 roadless acres. On the other side of the issue, off-road vehicle enthusiasts find the terrain especially challenging and would like to see as much of it as possible available for motorized recreation. Proximity to the Tri-Cities and the unique terrain help explain why up to 150 machines may be seen in the area on a warm weekend.

The overseeing Bureau of Land Management recommended against wilderness designation in an earlier review, but in 1981 thought they had devised a compromise plan. They designated 5,000 acres of the most unique and threatened land as an Outstanding Natural Area to be protected by strict year-round regulations. This area was to be off limits to off-road vehicle activity, which was to be confined to another designated 5,000 acres to the east. A one-half to one-mile-wide buffer zone would separate motorized recreation from the Natural Area and most adjacent privately owned farmland.

*Immediate right: In Washington the future of young ferruginous hawks like these depends on the recently protected habitat in the Juniper Dunes Wilderness. Dick Fitzner photo  Opposite page: Great Blazing Star, one of the grassland's vegetative treasures. Joel W. Rogers photo  Below: Rose Creek Preserve, a popular spot for Pullman area residents. Bess Hudson photo*

Washington's environmental community rejected the proposal as inadequate and farmers agreed the new plan had little prospect of stopping trespassing, noise, and vandalism. Supported by the National Audubon Society, Sierra Club, Washington Wilderness Coalition, and the local Friends of the Juniper Forest, preservationists held out for official wilderness designation. Finally in 1983 a proposal for a 7,140-acre wilderness was added to the Washington Wilderness Bill. In July 1984 Juniper Dunes Wilderness was officially designated as the Columbia Basin's first federal wilderness.

All efforts to save elements of Washington's natural heritage are not so controversial. In fact, the legislature recognized the need to preserve the state's natural diversity back in 1972 when the Natural Area Preserve Act was passed. This legislation was amended in 1981 to provide for an organized procedure for developing a Natural Area Preserve System to be managed by the Washington Natural Heritage Program. Today the Program coordinates efforts of private groups and government agencies as they work to identify and designate Natural Area Preserves. The state's 1983 Natural Heritage Plan identifies 64 such areas on state, federal, and private lands, 16 within the Columbia Basin. The Program has identified the Puget Trough and Columbia Basin as the physiographic provinces where elements of natural diversity have been most seriously jeopardized.

The Nature Conservancy, a national, non-profit, private conservation organization, initiated the Washington Natural Heritage Program in 1977. Since chartered in 1966 they have assisted in the preservation of thousands of acres of critical natural areas. "Land conservation through private action" is one of the mottoes of the Conservancy, which considers itself the real estate arm of the environmental movement. Using monies received from foundations and corporations as well as from individuals, they move in quickly with cash to buy threatened parcels of sensitive lands. They also accept donations of lands deemed worthy of preservation, and acquire conservation easements by which landowners agree to forego specific development rights indefinitely.

The Conservancy retains some of its preserves; others are conveyed to appropriate public or private conservation groups or educational institutions. As of 1983 they had 17 preserves in Washington, including seven within the Columbia Basin.

Along the north side of the Rattlesnake Hills east of Yakima is 14-acre Moxee Bog, a relict of the last Ice Age. South of Lind, 25-acre Lind Shrub-Steppe is one of the last and largest relatively pristine examples of the Big Sagebrush/Idaho fescue associations remaining in Eastern Washington. In northern Lincoln County, Magnuson Butte sticks above the surrounding Channeled Scabland, rising to an elevation of 3,000 feet. On the northeast face of its summit a remnant area of an Idaho fescue/snowberry vegetative community is protected in a 28-acre reserve. This once much more extensive habitat has been severely damaged by over-grazing and conversion of range to agricultural fields. The Moxee Bog and Magnuson Butte preserves can be visited only with prior permission, and the Lind site is closed because of its fragility, but some of the other preserves are open to the public. One of these is popular Rose Creek Preserve nestled in the rolling wheat fields north of Pullman. This 12-acre site protects rare Palouse riparian bottomland with its botanical remnant black hawthorn/cow parsnip association.

Even with a sizable budget, funds are too limited to allow the Nature Conservancy to purchase all sites that warrant protection. As an alternative to outright purchases, the Conservancy initiated its new Washington Landowner Contract and Natural Areas Registry Program in 1983. It is designed to reach landowners quickly and encourage voluntary protection for high priority areas identified by the Washington Natural Heritage Program. In 1983 almost 30 parcels totalling more than 600 acres, many in the Columbia Basin, were safeguarded.

The Nature Conservancy is a conservation organization geared to action. Here is where the environmental community puts its money where its mouth is. Within Washington alone the organization has helped set aside more than 8,000 acres of the state's vanishing natural diversity. Eighteen conservation-minded corporate associates including Washington Water Power, Rainier National Bank, and Weyerhaeuser have joined more than 7,000 members of the Washington Chapter of The Nature Conservancy. A modest annual dues of $10 entitles members to receive the national *Nature Conservancy News,* the quarterly *Washington Chapter Newsletter,* and invitations to field trips and other special events on Conservancy preserves. The mailing address for the Washington Field Office of The Nature Conservancy is 1601 Second Avenue, Suite 910, Seattle, Washington 98101.

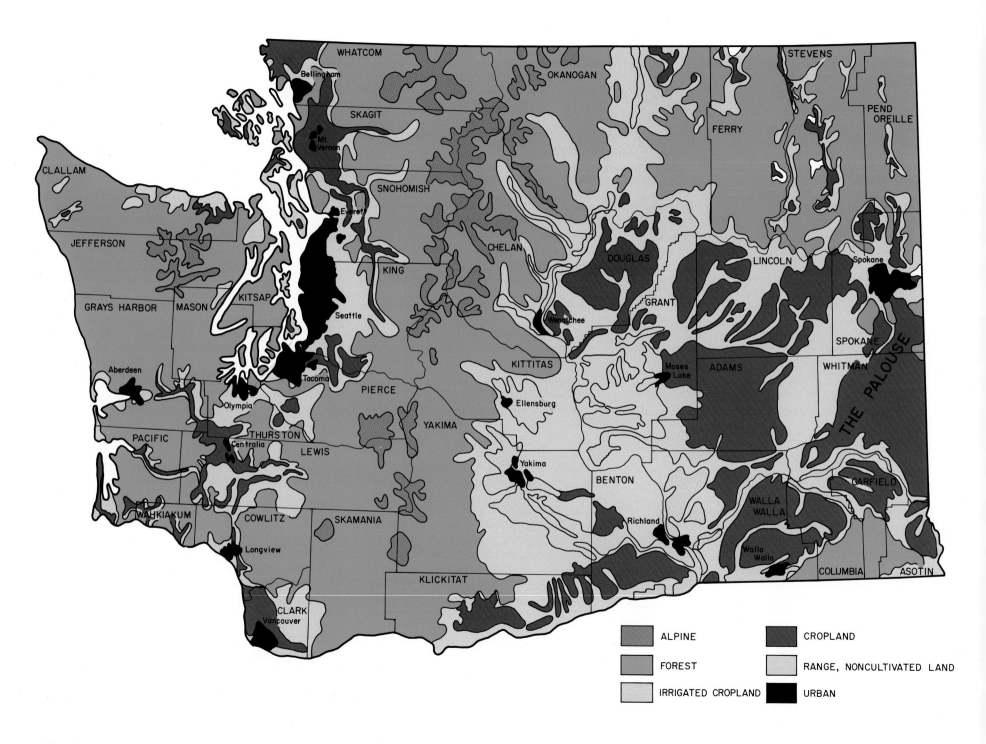

ALPINE

FOREST

IRRIGATED CROPLAND

CROPLAND

RANGE, NONCULTIVATED LAND

URBAN

Map left: Land Use in Washington. The state's agriculture, with its range, cropland, and irrigated cropland, blankets the Columbia Basin. Modified after WSU Extension Bulletin 703.

# AGRICULTURE
# Region by Region

Agriculture is Washington's number two industry, achieving a total value of production of $3 billion for the first time in 1981. This cornerstone of the state's economy is concentrated in Eastern Washington, inland from the Cascades. The region may only account for a third of the state's total area and just 20 percent of the population, but it includes 85 percent of the cropland and generates the lion's share of agricultural commodities.

An area that was once shrugged off as a useless wasteland, dubbed the Great Columbia Desert, is now a veritable agricultural horn of plenty, ranking as one of the nation's most bountiful farming districts. Production within the region ranks Washington as the nation's top grower of apples, hops, sweet cherries, dry peas, spearmint oil, lentils, and second ranking producer of potatoes, pears, grapes, apricots, green peas, asparagus, sweet corn (for processing) and prunes and plums. So rich are agricultural districts in some quarters that farm earnings in three area counties rank them in the top 50 of the nation's 3,072 counties.

*Left: One of Eastern Washington's many grainlands sentinels. John Alwin photo*

The region's agricultural landscape is surprisingly varied, ranging from the checkerboard fabric of emerald green, highly humanized irrigation districts, to vast expanses of sage and bunch grass rangelands, to often-photographed golden, rolling wheatlands.

On a general level most of agricultural Eastern Washington can be divided geographically into five major districts. Walla Walla Country is the oldest, and yet remains one of the most productive. Next door is the internationally renowned Palouse, the envy of grain farmers worldwide. The irrigated lands along the Yakima River to the west are equally famous for their prodigious bounty of fruits and vegetables. In the central Basin the more recently developed 500,000 irrigated acres of the Columbia Basin Project claim some of Washington's record yields. The arc-shaped Big Bend Country peripheral to the Project lands on the east and north is classic Eastern Washington grainland complete with wheat towns and sentinel-like grain elevators. Finally, to the northwest and spilling out of our Eastern Washington region is the Wenatchee Fruit District, long associated with its apple-scented air and big, juicy Delicious apples.

# WALLA WALLA COUNTRY

*Jose' duis Rowero and his family from Acapulco at work on Pierce's Green Valley onion farm west of Walla Walla. John Alwin photo*

Like most of Eastern Washington's agricultural regions, Walla Walla Country is an excellent example of a perceptual, or vernacular region. State highway maps don't locate or identify it by name, nor do roadside markers proclaim when you enter or leave. This is a region perceived to exist by past and present residents and by others outside the area. It is recognized as distinct from surrounding sections, possessing its own special, shared features.

Historically, the term, Walla Walla Country, was applied to the entire Columbia Basin. But before long the name singled out the section of Eastern Washington south of the Snake and between the Columbia River and the Blue Mountains. A long agricultural history and a strong regional focus on the town of Walla Walla remain shared traits of this belt of territory from Wallula to Pomeroy and between Starbuck and the Oregon line.

Walla Walla Country is the Columbia Basin's undisputed historic core. It was here that white settlement and agriculture first took root. The fertile bottomlands astride the Walla Walla River and the adjacent benchlands and hillsides were the first to prove the Basin's commercial potential for livestock grazing as well as irrigated and dryland farming. Techniques and methods tried and proven here were applied in subsequently settled areas of Eastern Washington.

Marcus Whitman, legendary Protestant missionary to the Cayuse tribe, is credited with planting the seeds of commercial farming in the Columbia Basin in the 1830s. By that time fur traders already had shown crops could be grown, at least adjacent to their riverside posts. At the minimum each establishment had a small garden spot that

provided fresh vegetables for post staff and perhaps passing brigades. The most ambitious project was initiated by the Hudson's Bay Company in the 1820s at Fort Colville on the Columbia just north of the Basin. Within a few years the plantings there merited the title of "farm," producing copious quantities of grain and vegetables as well as cattle for the Hudson's Bay Company's Columbia Department.

Fur traders also were the first farmers in the Walla Walla. Passing up-country in the fall of 1836 to establish Waiilatpu, Eastern Washington's first mission, Whitman and his fellow travellers witnessed the fur traders' Basin horticulture firsthand. Two miles east of the HBC's Fort Nez Perce, located at the mouth of the Walla Walla River, they passed by the post's planting of potatoes, pumpkins, onions, cucumbers, and melons, which one of the group described as "the best." This naturally pleased the mission group, since as well as hoping to Christianize area Indians, the Walla Walla missionaries also intended to help make them tillers of the soil. These productive HBC gardens reinforced the selection of the valley for the undertaking.

Fur trade garden plots involved company employees in producing agricultural commodities for a closed corporate system. Whitman hoped to initiate Eastern Washington's first family farms. The location chosen for the mission was consistent with that objective, a place Whitman thought had "far more good land for cultivation . . . than at any place in the upper Columbia."

In 1837 Whitman sowed 12 acres of corn and planted additional ground in potatoes, peas, barley, and apples at the riverside mission 25 miles east of Fort Nez Perce. His irrigated crops flourished in the rich alluvial soils, and cultivated area was increased. By at least 1841 the rewards of horticulture were obvious and Indians began farming their own small gardens and fields.

Whitman's untimely death in 1847 and the subsequent hostilities between Indians and whites may have put a temporary hold on agricultural expansion, but the 1858 lifting of a military ban on settlers let loose a surging mass of Walla Walla-bound farmers. By the late summer of 1859, 800 had settled in the valley. The 1860 census shows this pioneer farming cluster in the Walla Walla lowland already included 6,902 acres of "improved

land in farms." All this at a time when the rest of Eastern Washington remained the domain of Indians, fur traders, and jack rabbits.

The presence of hundreds of soldiers and mounts at the army's Fort Walla Walla established a few miles from the Whitman Mission in 1856, meant a home market for agricultural products and provided a nucleus for town formation. Coincidental to the reoccupation of the Walla Walla, discovery of rich placer gold deposits in the Northwest and Northern Rockies provided rapidly expanding markets. The young, but precocious, community of Walla Walla quickly assumed the role of regional metropolis and distribution center to a vast 100,000-square-mile section of the interior Northwest.

Local demand for agricultural products grew with the town and the hordes of miners passing through headed up- and down-country. One estimate suggests 30,000 people passed through Walla Walla in 1862 alone! Oats found a ready market among freighters serving the peripheral mining camps, and barrels of flour milled from local wheat, as well as vegetables and beef, could be marketed in these mining centers at handsome profits. Apples reportedly fetched as much as one dollar apiece. Heightened agricultural demand pushed the Walla Walla farmers' frontier outward, even up onto previously shunned hillsides. By 1870 the Walla Walla valley largely was filled and constituted Washington's most extensive farming district.

When markets in mountain mining centers to the north, east, and south declined by the late '60s, area farmers looked to the west and expansion of markets reached via the Columbia River. The Walla Walla-Wallula Road soon was clogged with freight teams hauling the region's bounty to awaiting flat-bottomed sternwheelers that would ferry it down the Columbia to Portland and export to world markets.

*Above: Pomeroy, at the eastern end of the Walla Walla, is a true grain town. John Alwin photo*

*Right: Productive grainlands, like these northeast of Dayton, dominate the eastern section of the Walla Walla. John Alwin photo*

Heavy traffic along this transport link led to construction of Washington's first rail line. In 1875 the Walla Walla and Columbia River Railroad Company initiated through service on its narrow gauge Walla Walla-Wallula line. Without direct access to rail service farmers in the Walla Walla Country's northern section near the Snake River relied on ingenious chutes and conveyor systems to pass grain down the steep canyon walls to the awaiting river boats. Agriculturally the Walla Walla Country had led the way in commercial farming and production for export markets. Other Eastern Washington farming districts followed suit.

In total dollar value of agricultural products, the Walla Walla Country has slipped below Eastern Washington's much newer, massive irrigated Yakima Project and Columbia Basin Project areas, but remains one of Washington's and the Northwest's major agricultural regions.

Walla Walla, Columbia, and Garfield counties generally are considered Walla Walla Country, but the former accounts for over half the farm acreage and fully 80 percent of market value of agricultural products. One-hundred-fifty years of farming have left a visible mark on the county. Among all counties in the 11 Far West states, only neighboring Whitman in the Palouse has a higher percentage of its land in crops. The 76 percent of Walla Walla County devoted to crops ranges from irrigated onion fields at 500 feet elevation in the Walla Walla River Valley up to dryland grain fields on the 3,500-foot flank of the Blue Mountains.

Even though agriculturally Walla Walla is synonymous with onions in the minds of most Americans, this pungent vegetable is grown on just 1,100 of the region's 1,000,000 acres of cropland. Even within Washington, Grant County produces more onions each year than Walla Walla County, and the Adams County harvest is about equal.

Walla Walla Country remains dominantly wheat country. Its 400,000 acres rank it as one of the nation's major wheat districts. Excellent crop years like those in 1983 and 1984 can reward farmers with non-irrigated yields of 100 or more bushels per acre.

Columbia and Garfield counties are mainly dryland grain producing districts. On this sweeping and dramatically sculpted north flank of the Blue Mountains, wheat or barley, followed by a year of fallow has been standard for generations. Lately county agents and other conservationists concerned about soil erosion have been pushing a three-year crop rotation (wheat:barley:fallow) where moisture conditions permit.

Historically, Columbia County's agricultural base has been somewhat more diversified than its neighbor to the east, and in that respect more like Walla Walla County. Peas, both dry edible and green, have a long history in the area. Green peas, a non-irrigated crop grown in rotation with wheat, have dominated, and as recently as 1978 covered almost 19,000 acres. This was Green Giant Country. Until the late 1970s Green Giant operated a large pea processing plant in Dayton. Each spring a 300-foot-tall Green Giant sprouted from the hillside above town where employees had fertilized an area in the shape of the jolly green man. By 1980 the area planted in green peas in Columbia County had plummeted to just 4,100 acres. Pea processing continued just across the county line at Smith Canning and Freezing's Waitsburg plant, but in Dayton, Green Giant's neatly landscaped plant handles only asparagus.

Much greater irrigated acreage and sections with up to 220 freeze-free days permit a more diversified agricultural economy in Walla Walla County. In addition to top ranking wheat and barley on more than 300,000 acres, are extensive acreages in hay, green peas, dry edible peas, potatoes, asparagus, and orchards, especially apples. Smaller plantings of onions, sweet corn, lettuce, spinach, carrots, squash, and radishes help maintain the area's reputation as a vegetable producer.

## WALLA WALLA SWEETS

Gourmet chefs know of and demand them, and nationwide, people order 20-pound gift boxes from local distributors through ads in *Sunset, Cook's Magazine,* and other periodicals—Walla Walla Sweets, you don't even have to say onions. This vegetable may not be the Walla Walla Country's number one crop in value or acreage, but it is synonymous with the district worldwide. Other growers in Washington may advertise their's as Walla Walla Sweets but, according to Stan Myers of the Walla Walla Gardener's Association, only the Walla Walla Valley produces the classic juicy and flavorful big onion that can be eaten like an apple.

Research by Joe E. Locati, former District Horticultural Inspector for the Washington Department of Agriculture, shows the Walla Walla Sweet's lineage goes back to French farmers on the Mediterranean island of Corsica. His investigation suggests the variety was brought into the valley around the turn of the century by a former French army soldier who had served on the island. It quickly was adopted by the area's large contingent of Italian horticulturists who referred to it as the French onion. Its classic onion shape, unique combination of mild flavor, sweetness, and early maturing nature made it an immediate marketplace success.

Imaginative sleuthing by Locati traces the Walla Walla Sweet name to the 1950s and a local shipper who placed recipes for a "Walla Walla Sweet Onion Sandwich" in the bottom of his sacks of jumbo-size onions.

# PALOUSE

The evening view from atop Steptoe Butte at the height of harvest season affords one of the most dramatic visual introductions to the Palouse. In all directions the headlights of distant combines and grain trucks can be seen bobbing and weaving in and out of sight as they navigate the rolling hills. The region's highways carry a steady stream of trucks scurrying back and forth between field and elevator. Night and day grain dust fills the air to the dismay of allergy sufferers. On hundreds of farms and in communities from Mockonema, Fallon, and Cashup (which don't even appear on state highway maps), to regional metropolises like Pullman and Colfax, the sights and sounds of harvest dominate. For several weeks each summer this is a region with just one thing on its mind—reaping the bounty of the nation's most productive dryland grain crop.

In spite of the Palouse's international notoriety not everyone agrees on its geographical boundaries. Researchers and residents alike seem to have their own notions of what areas should and should not be gathered in under the Palouse banner. There is a Palouse Empire Mall in Moscow, Colfax is the site for the annual Palouse Empire Fair, and Rockford is home to Palouse Seed Company, but would a Palouse Drive-In at Dayton or a Palouse Drug in Washtucna make sense?

A quarter century ago University of Idaho geography professor Harry Caldwell suggested the unadorned term, Palouse, be restricted to a core area of maximum agreement. His map shows approximately 70 percent of the region lies in Whitman County north of the Snake and east of the Palouse River. The remainder is divided about equally between a section of Spokane County southeast of

*Left: Travellers on the Palouse-Pullman Highway are immersed in a sea of golden grain fields. John Alwin photo*

Above: Elevator man, Eric Swanson, takes time off between grain truck arrivals.

Above right: Palouse gold.

Right: Three combines etch the geometry of harvest on grainland south of Spangle. John Alwin photos

*Closely manicured fields north of Pullman. Forest-crowned Rockies of northern Idaho rise in the distance. John Alwin photo*

Cheney (Rockford-Fairfield-Spangle area) and the sliver-like, western farming fringe of Latah County across the border in neighboring Idaho. The Washington part of this Palouse appears as a contiguous cropland area on the land use map at the start of this section.

The Palouse is an agricultural region *extraordinaire*. Its farming muscle is reflected in statistics for Whitman County, which comprises the bulk of the area. Year in and year out Whitman produces more wheat than any other county in the nation, consistently rewarding farmers with two to three times the average national yield per acre. In most years this one county produces almost a quarter of Washington's wheat, the state's leading crop. And wheat isn't the only crop harvested from the fertile rolling hill country. Whitman County also

accounts for one-third of the state's barley, more than one-half of Washington's dry edible peas, and approximately three-quarters of its lentils.

Phenomenal productivity has motivated farmers to expand their fields into every possible nook and cranny. As a consequence, nowhere else in the American Far West does cropland so dominate a county. With about 80 percent of its land devoted to crop production, Whitman is the most farmed county in the eleven-state Far West area. It ranks in the top 50 of the nation's 3,072 counties in total farm earnings, and moves even higher when that amount is calculated on a per farm average among Whitman's 1,225 farms.

The rise of the Palouse to agricultural pre-eminence would not have surprised Isaac Stevens, Washington Territory's first governor. Crossing a

section in the spring of 1855 enroute to today's Montana, Stevens wrote, "I will again say, we have been astonished to-day at the luxuriance of the grass and the richness of the soil. The whole view present to the eye a vast bed of flowers in all their varied beauty. The country is a rolling tableland, and the soil like that of the prairies of Illinois . . ." Within 25 short years this fertile hill country had begun to resemble the productive farming districts of longer-settled Illinois.

Cattlemen had preceded the farmers into the Palouse as they had in other quarters of Eastern Washington. By the late 1850s resolution of Indian-white hostilities and prospects for quick profit in the not-too-distant mining centers had begun to lure cattlemen onto the Basin's grassy expanses. These former Indian lands were public domain, unfenced and free for the using. Palouse country grass—lush, tall, and nutritious—was especially prized. Some quick profits were made during this open range period, but it proved to be a brief and transitory phase in the agrarian occupance.

By the early 1870s the industry was in marked decline. A few ranchers remained, but the range cattle industry left little more than severely overgrazed grassland in its wake. It did not promote a dense network of towns or transport facilities. Cattlemen preferred wide open spaces devoid of people and competing land uses and, since cattle transported themselves to market, trails were all that were necessary. As Palouse cattle numbers dwindled, sheep increased and by 1880 had displaced cattle as the most important element in Whitman County livestock. These were times of swift and dramatic change in the Palouse and soon sheepmen found themselves being elbowed out by a rush of eager homesteaders.

River valleys were the first to pass to these new agrarian landowners since access to water, timber, and potential hayland were of paramount concern to frontier farmers. Growth was initially both particular and hesitant with habitation discontinuous and largely restricted to riverside stringers. It was along waterways that the region's first towns developed. The Palouse River community of Colfax, incorporated in 1873, was the earliest. More widespread occupance of the Palouse had to await the late-1870s realization that previously shunned hillsides would, after all, reward farmers with prodigious wheat yields. This discovery triggered a true-West land rush that guaranteed the new federal land office in Colfax a "land-office" business. A U.S. Army Corps of Engineers lieutenant exploring the entire Upper Columbia region in 1881 speculated that this young town at the junction of the north and south forks of the Palouse was "destined to become quite a railroad and commercial center . . ." The surrounding Palouse country was described as "nearly all of good quality, and . . . being rapidly filled." He estimated that not more than a tenth of the land had been "taken up and occupied," yet by the close of the decade the region was filled.

Taking advantage of the Homestead Act and other land acts, optimistic settlers filed on 160- and 320-acre parcels and took up their new residence on the frontier. Initial years were almost always difficult. For some their first home was a dugout carved into the slope of a hill. Others made do with crude wooden shacks and the fortunate few with ready access to ponderosa pine could build somewhat more substantial log structures. The virgin bunch grass proved difficult to break, equipment was in short supply, and transportation essential to convey agricultural commodities to market was difficult and expensive, or non-existent.

During the decade of the 1880s the appearance of a new element in the geography of the Palouse all but assured its continued growth and future prosperity. The 1884 extension of a Northern Pacific Railroad line to Colfax, with other carriers and branch lines following in quick succession, constituted nothing less than a transportation revolution. Rail service unlocked the agricultural bounty of this phenomenally rich region. Overnight, settlers had direct rail access and even the option of hiring their own immigrant cars right to the Palouse. Goods, supplies, and equipment could be hauled in more easily and economically, and agricultural products shipped out with a minimum of trouble. Through promotional schemes and boomer literature, the railroads, eager to settle the land with farmers who would generate traffic for their lines, lured even more homesteaders into the wheatlands.

Increased population soon was reflected in an expanded network of towns and villages. In 1890 the new towns of Palouse City (population 1,119), Rockford (644), and Farmington (418) each had a flour mill and some boasted newspapers, banks, and populations greater than today. By the late 1880s Whitman County's 2,300 highly productive farms already had attracted national attention.

Over the last century changes in Palouse agriculture have mirrored those of American agriculture with fewer, but larger farms, increasing dependence on mechanization, and more scientific methods. Average Whitman County farm size has increased each census year since 1890. That year's 286-acre average climbed to 384 in 1910, 532 in 1940, 913 by 1969, and according to the most recent Census of Agriculture, reached 1,143 acres in 1982. While average size has ballooned, total number of farms has dropped. The county's 2,350 farms in 1890 expanded to a 1910 peak of 3,096 and then began a steady decline, dropping in each census to the current 1,225. One by one smaller, non-economic operations were forced out of business. Cropland invariably was gobbled up by neighbors eager for the additional ground necessary to keep them economically viable in progressively larger-scale Palouse agriculture.

Greater mechanization, with its speed and efficiency, has gone hand-in-hand with the changing scale of farming. The turn-of-the-century arrival of horse-drawn combines was one landmark development. Huge, specially designed hillside, or levelling, combines were soon synonymous with the Palouse. Even today's giant, four-wheel drive tractors could not have rivaled the visual impact of one of the massive combines as it was pulled over golden Palouse wheatlands by straining horse and mule teams of up to 20, 30, or more head.

*Palouse City Roller Mills, Palouse, circa 1889. By the '80s railside communities like this were essential to the agricultural occupance of surrounding land. Washington State University Library photo*

# LANDSCAPE METEOROLOGY

By the 1880s, outsiders were perplexed at how the Palouse and some other sections of the Columbia Basin could so consistently produce such high, non-irrigated wheat yields. How was it possible in a region assumed to be rainless at the least, and at best, plagued by a predictable summer drought? The federal government ordered an investigation of this confusing anomaly in 1885 and placed Lieutenant Frank Greene of the Signal Corps in charge.

A standard late-1880s explanation called upon the recently plowed ground, tree plantings, and new rail and telegraph lines to explain this apparent paradox. Strange as it sounds today, a century ago it was assumed such people-induced changes in the landscape enhanced productivity by triggering more precipitation. Victorians believed the mere process of settling rainfall deficit areas and converting the land to agricultural use caused the climate to become less dry, thus permitting consistently high yields.

"Trees bring rain" was one of the widespread beliefs of the time. In grassland areas like the Palouse, shade trees and orchards were thought to feed the clouds by enriching them with water vapor. Trees transpire, the theory explained, releasing moisture into the atmosphere, their shade lessens evaporation and buffets winds, and litter they shed acts as a sponge retaining even more moisture.

*Heading grain in the Palouse Country near Colfax. Horse power remained an integral part of agriculture well into the 20th century. Washington State University Library photo*

Plowed fields also were assumed to enhance precipitation. When hard, compact virgin grassland was plowed people thought its absorbtive power was so greatly enhanced that fields became gigantic storage reservoirs, soaked with water that could be released gradually to charge the atmosphere and produce precipitation. Nationally, it was common knowledge that "rain follows the plow."

Moisture also could be augmented, it was thought, by any means that facilitated the exchange of electrical charges between clouds and ground. Tall trees, acting as lightning rods, were seen as desirable, but could not rival the electrical conductivity of the new railroads' twin ribbons of iron and the wire of telegraph lines. Enough miles of both could rectify the electrical imbalance, and thus moisture shortfall, of just about anyplace.

Lieutenant Greene's 1888 report called upon more modern scientific findings to explain the high and consistent wheat yields. He cited a list of favorable characteristics including soil with great natural fertility and high moisture retention, mild winters, low intensity rainfall, and dry ripening and harvest seasons as important pluses. Whatever the reasons, Palouse farmers already had come to expect bumper crops by the late 1880s.

*Impressive horse-drawn combines like this one navigating steep hillsides became synonymous with the Palouse. Eastern Washington State Historical Society photo*

Other machinery innovations followed in quick succession, many incorporating gasoline engines to provide power formerly supplied by horses. Better and larger plows, cultivators, and other equipment, as well as new varieties of wheat, additional crops, herbicides, and pesticides all have contributed to the transformation of agrarian life.

Except for a few years during and immediately after World War II, wheat has been king of Palouse agriculture. For a century, soft winter wheat has dominated. It is fall-sown after the harvest, usually following a good rain. Winter wheats can be grown only in regions with distinct, but somewhat moderated winters. If too cold, plants winter-kill. If too mild, wheat grows but produces no grain. The Palouse area's mild, yet distinct winter is an exemplary winter wheat environment.

Palouse soft winter wheat is a commodity for export, with about 90 percent destined for overseas markets. Because of its low gluten content it is unsuitable for leavened breads, but is excellent for flat breads and pasta. Pacific Rim Asian nations have been major customers, and recently new export markets have been developed in the Middle East. In nations from South Korea to Japan, the Phillipines, Taiwan, India, Egypt, and Yemen, flour ground from Palouse wheat is used to make flat breads, cookies, cakes, and noodles. If Chinese fears of the disease TKC smut can by allayed, the billion-plus citizens of the People's Republic of China might become an important market for Eastern Washington wheat.

Winter wheat usually is seeded between late September and mid-October, when temperatures are still in the 40- to 60-degree range. In average years subsequent weather stays mild enough for seeds to sprout and start growing. Seedlings continue to grow into November, benefiting from the onset of the area's wet season. Above ground growth of small plants stops at about a four-inch height with the arrival of colder weather, but root development continues through much of the winter. With the arrival of warmer and still relatively wet spring days, plants experience vigorous growth and by early August wheat ripens and turns golden, ready for the combines. Predictably dry, warm, and sunny Palouse summer days are ideal for wheat harvesting.

According to Extension Agent Clint Luce, annual precipitation within Whitman County increases in a regular progression from west to east, "adding an inch of rainfall for every 100 feet of elevation almost exactly." On the drier western fringe of the Palouse where precipitation averages less than 15 inches, summer-fallow is standard practice. In most years this semiarid hill country adjacent to the Scablands receives inadequate moisture for growing dryland grain in the same field year after year. By leaving land fallow, or unplowed, in alternate years and cultivating or using herbicides to control weeds, soil moisture builds up and helps assure a better crop the subsequent year. Farmers around Hay and Endicott like to say, "It takes two years to grow a crop."

Like their counterparts throughout the Palouse, farmers in this driest quarter commonly include barley in their crop rotation. This small grain has been an important part of area agriculture since the homesteading era. Now, as in the past, its primary use is for animal feed, today mostly for livestock outside the region. Some also is used in the beer industry, finding its way into familiar brews from Milwaukee to Olympia. Barley rewards farmers with high yields and provides them with a degree of diversification.

Since farmers here crop only half their land in any one year and yields are lower than in wetter areas to the east, farms tend to be the largest in the Palouse. An economic-sized unit is above the 1,100- to 1,200-acre Palouse average.

Farther east, higher up the flank of the Columbia Basin, farming practices gradually yield to a three-year rotation scheme. In this 15- to 19-inch rainfall area of central Whitman County and a small section of Spokane County, higher average annual precipitation allows dryland crops to be grown two out of three years. Around the communities of Colfax, Dusty, St. John, Rosalia, and

*Time out for a photograph for these early-day Palouse field hands. Eastern Washington State Historical Society photo*

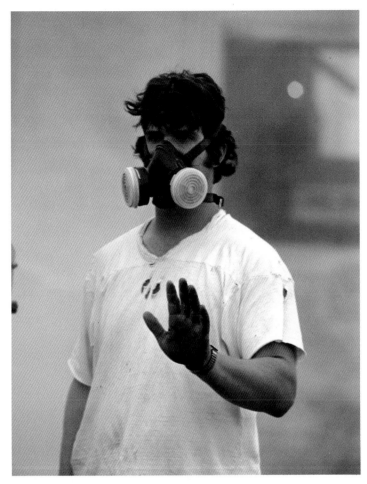

*Above left: Ever-present grain dust at a Spangle elevator requires employee, Robert Walker, to take appropriate precautions. Above: Early morning grain truck approaches for weigh-in at the Fallon elevator north of Pullman. Left: Harvest already exceeds storage at Fallon, and more on the way. Far left: In echelon combines make short order of the 100-bushel-per-acre winter wheat harvest on the Robert Kramer farm outside Colfax. John Alwin photos*

*Brothers Mark and Greg Mader prepare their giant machines for the harvest on their 2,500-acre family grain farm. The combine in the foreground can cut up to 1,000 bushels per hour with its 24-foot cutting platform. John Alwin photo*

## A CAPITAL INVESTMENT

An average early-1980s value of $2,500 per acre in the central and eastern sections of the Palouse means a land book value of over $2,500,000 for the average-size farm. Machinery and equipment are an additional large investment. According to Franklin Ott of Fairfield's Saunders & Ott, which bills itself as "Fairfield's Largest International Harvester Dealer" (Fairfield's population is 601), new machinery costs an additional $400,000. That figure includes a hillside combine ($175,000), plow ($17,000), cultivator ($16,000), harrow with cart ($8,000), set of drills ($30,000), windrower for peas ($30,000), at least one grain-hauling truck ($30,000), obligatory pick-up truck ($10,000), and equally necessary shop tools and machinery ($5,000). A new 250 horsepower, four-wheel drive tractor, now preferred by most farmers over crawler-types long synonymous with Palouse farming, adds the remaining $75,000.

Sprague, farmers routinely follow a wheat:barley:summer-fallow rotation. Since crops can be produced on two-thirds of a farmer's fields each year, farms here tend to be somewhat smaller than those to the west, around the Palouse average.

In the wetter eastern fringe of this intermediate rainfall area some farmers have incorporated dry edible peas and lentils into their crop rotation. Peas were introduced into the Palouse around the time of World War I. They were readily accepted by farmers who often grew them as a replacement to summer-fallow. Americans know these peas as those we consume in split-pea soup. Most of the large Palouse crop is shipped overseas where peas are rehydrated by soaking and sold as canned peas, especially popular in England and Brazil.

Lentils are an extremely high-protein (22 to 34 percent) crop introduced into the Palouse in the 1920s. The record is sketchy, but evidently a German, Seventh-Day Adventist minister in the Farmington area of northeastern Whitman County was the first to grow the crop. Since Adventists are vegetarians, high-protein vegetables are essential in diets. Initial production was local and for consumption of family and friends, but by the 1930s crop success had motivated other Palouse farmers to begin incorporating lentils in their rotation. Acreage remained small until the late 1950s and early 1960s when export markets were developed. Today 80 percent of the crop is exported, much to the Middle East and South America. Increased international competition, especially from Canada and Turkey, and insect problems have reduced acreage over the last several years.

For generations dry peas and lentils have played an important role in area farming. As legumes, both vegetables have beneficial root bacteria nodules that take atmospheric nitrogen and fix it in the soil. They are thus able to supply a large percentage of their own nitrogen needs, important in this somewhat nitrogen-deficient soil. Some residual nitrogen also remains in soil for subsequent wheat or barley crops, and research is now under way to find ways of boosting remnant amounts of this critical plant nutrient. Since both are non-cereal crops their planting breaks disease, insect, and weed cycles that multiply in a grain-only rotation.

*Combine spits spring barley into awaiting grain-hauling truck. John Alwin photo*

East of a north-south line approximated by U.S. Highway 195, annual cropping prevails. Periods of summer-fallow usually are unnecessary in this wettest section of the Palouse where yearly precipitation exceeds 19 inches. Precipitation continues to increase with elevation in an easterly direction reaching as high as 24 inches along the state line and even higher in adjacent sections of Idaho. Both winter wheat and barley remain important crops, but the sub-humid conditions, coupled with fertile soil, mean other crops also do extremely well. Peas and lentils become more common and continue to gain in importance farther east in Idaho, earning Moscow the title of "Dry Pea and Lentil Capital of the World."

Next time you seed a lawn chances are good you will use one of the Palouse area's lesser known commodities—Bluegrass seed. The more humid eastern section of Washington's Palouse, *not* the Bluegrass State, produces most of the nation's Kentucky Bluegrass seed. Turf grass seed acreage is concentrated in the upper Palouse area of southeastern Spokane County. There, luxuriant perennial grasses mantle tens of thousands of rolling acres around Rockford, Fairfield, and eastward into the Idaho Panhandle. Smaller acreages are scattered about the eastern section of Whitman County and outside the Palouse, south of the Snake River in the Pomeroy area. According to Gary Storment of Dye Seed Ranch, one of several

area seed companies, demand goes hand-in-hand with the nation's home-building activity. Recent high interest rates for home construction have reduced demand for this unique Palouse crop.

Despite an unblemished history of not a single total crop failure in the region's century-plus agricultural history, some Palouse farmers are eager for greater crop diversity. This is nothing new. Apples were the hot new crop around the turn of the century. Orchards were planted on slopes amid the wheat fields, especially in the wetter eastern sections. Farmers were told theirs would soon be the nation's premier apple-growing region. The remnant and now aged orchards on the lower flank of Steptoe Butte and other hillsides are all that remain of the short-lived Palouse apple boom.

Modern-day efforts at crop diversification are more scientific and economically sound, but even they come with no guarantees. Recent efforts at cultivating chick peas, rapeseed, sunflowers, safflower, and even lupine have met with only varying degrees of success.

The Palouse has evolved into almost a crop-only agricultural region with livestock now less important than at any other time. A comparison of 1910 and 1982 figures for Whitman County clearly shows that diminished role. Cattle fared best over the years, holding about equal number-wise, but never numerous enough to rank the county in the state's top dozen. Sheep numbers declined to less than one-tenth the 1910 figure, the dairy herd plummeted from 9,300 to 273, and hogs, long synonymous with Palouse livestock, numbered just one-third the 1910 figure. Despite the decline, Whitman still has more hogs than any other Washington county. As in the past, locally produced barley and wheat provide excellent feed, and cull peas an important protein supplement.

An overwhelming cropping emphasis and expansion of cropland over most of the Palouse Hills have exacted a tremendous environmental toll. For decades the Palouse has had the dubious distinction of having one of the nation's most serious soil erosion problems. When the Secretary of Agriculture speaks on the evils of soil loss and the need for national conservation programs, he singles out the Palouse by name. Grain grower Robert Kramer, who farms 1,100 acres just west of Colfax,

*Paul Schluneger loads his 1,250-bushel-capacity rig with on-farm stored grain for the 33-mile trip to Almota on the Snake and downriver shipment by barge. John Alwin photo*

*Sunflowers have been tried as an alternative crop by some Palouse farmers. WSU photo*

feels erosion is "terrible, it's very bad." Thirty-year veteran Whitman County Extension Agent, Clint Luce, thinks erosion remains "very serious" and ranks as "our major problem in farming right now."

There was a time when the Palouse Hills' mantle of native bunch grass with its deep and inter-twined network of roots held soil in place, even on steepest 50-degree slopes. Conversion of virgin prairie into cultivated fields destroyed the binding grass cover laying ground bare and susceptible to accelerated erosion. Research suggests Palouse soil loss is especially severe on steep, fallow ground in late winter and early spring. Heavy rain during this critical one- to two-month period comes when ground is partially frozen and unable to absorb moisture. Water from melting snow and precipitation that falls runs down steep slopes picking up surface soil, washing it into gullies and streams and eventually the muddy Palouse River. Deep rivulets and gullies eaten into hillsides testify to the erosive power of the draining water. Erosion tends to be highest in summer-fallow areas where annual soil loss can reach 100 to 200 tons per acre. A Palouse average annual loss of close to 30 tons of soil per acre is among the nation's highest.

Like everyone else, Palouse farmers are crea-tures of habit; old and engrained ways of doing things die hard. But days may be numbered for those farmers planning to maximize immediate returns for "just one more year." If the Palouse is to be a national resource for future generations, some immediate profits may have to be sacrificed and proven soil conservation practices adopted to protect this irreplaceable land that has produced so prodigiously for so long.

## PALOUSE SOIL EROSION

Harshest critics accuse Palouse farmers of mining and exporting topsoil and fear the eventual loss of this unique national resource. On a long-term basis, such fears may not be unfounded. In Whitman County studies have documented a decades-long average loss of 1,400 pounds of topsoil for *each* bushel of wheat produced. In some years this figure has exceeded two tons per bushel. Running water and tillage erosion, soil moved downhill merely by cultivating steep fields, have stripped up to two feet of soil in a single generation. Since even the deepest Palouse topsoil is only about 24 inches thick, current rates of loss are grave.

People commonly speak imprecisely about Palouse soil, often claiming depths of more than 100 feet. In truth, the combined thick-ness of the thin, upper soil layer and the much thicker underlying loess may total 100 feet. By definition soil is the product of a living environment involving chemical and physical changes of parent material from which it is derived, in this case the loess. On a scale of human time this is such a long-term process that soil is considered a non-renewable natural resource. In the Palouse the rate of soil destruction greatly exceeds the rate of soil-forming processes.

The cumulative effect of soil loss most easily is seen on the tops of many Palouse hills which now are noticeably lighter colored. Sometimes called clay knobs by locals, such hilltops are sites where deep erosion has stripped away productive top-soil, exposing less fertile subsoil with lower organic matter content. Soil destruction already has impacted crop yields, with low-est production (one-third the yield of non-eroded soils) coming from the most eroded slopes.

There is not a farmer in the Palouse who wouldn't prefer to keep topsoil in the fields and out of gullies and streams. Still, anyone who fails to adopt the best management practices is adding to the problem. In-creasing numbers of farmers are realizing that unless conservation practices are em-ployed on a wide basis, the region may face a bleak future of falling yields and the threat of unwanted federal regulations trig-gered by serious farm-caused water pollution.

A growing number of Palouse agricul-turalists are incorporating new soil-saving management practices. One key is to keep land continuously cropped whenever pos-sible since any cover is better than none at controlling water erosion. As one grain grower said, "the best method thus far is just to keep it in crop annually and have no summer-fallow." Rotation schemes and government programs that call for idled land intensify the soil erosion problem.

A wide range of soil-saving practices are available. Farmers in southeastern Spokane County have greatly reduced soil loss by mimicking the area's natural vegetation with thousands of acres of Kentucky Blue-grass. When market conditions permit, this perennial grass remains in a field for up to ten years. Farmers are rewarded with marketable grass seed, virtual elimination of soil erosion, and replenished soil organic matter.

Operators also can opt for divided slope, a time-proven method of reducing the amount of soil lost to water erosion. With this practice, hills are divided into two or three concentric zones with different crops in each zone, creating a bull's-eye pattern when viewed from above. Divided slope coupled with contour tillage helps slow run-off, reducing both soil and water loss. Greater difficulty in laying out fields and in working them discourages some farmers from adopting the practice. Maintaining grass cover on obvious hillside waterways is yet another proven way to reducing soil loss.

No-till and minimum tillage are among the newest management tools in the battle against soil destruction. No-till farming dispenses with deep tillage and overturning of the soil. With such plowless farming, fields are seeded through the undisturbed residues of the previous crop. Retention of a stubble mulch helps bind and protect soil from erosion as well as enhance water retention. Minimum soil disturbance reduces soil pulverization, limiting erosion and helping to maintain water absorption. If sufficient water can be retained the need for the bare ground of summer-fallow can be eliminated.

Few Palouse farmers have opted for no-till, perhaps in part because when soil is frozen even more water can run off fields. A greater number are experimenting with, or incorporating, minimum tillage. Stubble from a previous crop might only be knocked down, and summer-fallow treated with herbicides and cultivated only twice instead of several times. Such practices contrast markedly with the ritual of burning stubble at the end of each summer, a tradition still followed by some Palouse farmers.

*Opposite page: Stubble mulch is one effective means of reducing soil erosion. John Alwin photo*

*Left: Muddy Palouse Falls discharges water loaded with fertile Palouse soil. WSU photo*

# ALONG THE YAKIMA

The great Yakima Chief Kamiakin could not have known in the 1850s that his tiny irrigated garden in the Ahtanum Valley would be the precursor of today's sprawling half-million-acre irrigated cornucopia strung out over a distance of 175 miles. Earlier evidence of Indian irrigation with its ditches and control structures is sketchy, and Chief Kamiakin generally is credited with the Yakima Basin's first irrigation project. Sometime in the 1850s, evidently with the help of a priest at nearby Ahtanum Mission, he oversaw the construction of a quarter-mile-long ditch for diverting water from an Ahtanum tributary to a garden near his home. Arrival of white settlers beginning the next decade and their progressively larger irrigation projects soon engulfed Kamiakin's small plot and thousands of additional acres. In a span of one person's life, the transformation begun by the legendary chief saw the Yakima country's dry, sagebrush-covered valleys blossom into one of the nation's most productive agricultural regions.

Irrigated farming began slowly in the Yakima Basin and at least initially took a back seat to livestock grazing. With lucrative markets for beef at Seattle and to the north in the Okanogan mines of British Columbia, cattlemen moved herds into the Yakima and Kittitas valleys in the 1860s. The better-watered upper sections of both provided nutritious bunch grass as well as tall riverside rye grass.

As most Yakima-area school children learn, Fielding M. Thorp was the first white settler of record to take up residence in the valley. In late 1860 he drove a herd of more than 250 head of cattle into the Moxee area, and the following year built along the Yakima River opposite the mouth

*Fall colors light up the Yakima Valley fruit district below the Rattlesnake Hills. John Alwin photo*

*Above: Valley wine grape harvest requires abundant hand labor. Above right: Along Lateral A south of Yakima. Far right: Peaches, peaches, peaches! Right: Corn harvest on the Robert Riddle farm in the Kittitas. John Alwin photos*

of Ahtanum Creek. Others primarily interested in the stock business followed, spreading their herds over suitable sections of both the Yakima and Kittitas. For a short period, herds trailed over Snoqualmie and Naches passes to Puget Sound or north to the Okanogan mines fetched high prices.

Agriculture in both valleys remained overwhelmingly stock raising until the 1880s, but even as early as the late 1860s industrious farmers were proving the benefits of irrigated cropping. Kamiakin's garden already had shown that the fertile volcanic and river-derived soils of this assumed wasteland needed only water to be productive. Between the mid-Sixties and early Seventies modest water diversions from the Naches, Yakima, and Ahtanum in the upper Yakima Valley, and Manastash and Taneum creeks in the Kittitas Valley had converted former sage flats into garden spots. By 1870 at least a thousand acres were under irrigation in the Yakima Valley alone. Throughout the Seventies and into the Eighties cooperative efforts led to the formation of canal companies along the Yakima River. They undertook ever more ambitious enterprises, building historic canals, some of which are still carrying a century later.

Arrival of the Northern Pacific Railroad in Yakima City (Union Gap) in 1884, and two years later in Ellensburg, ushered in a new agrarian phase. Just as rails unlocked the agricultural bounty of the Palouse, so too, did the Iron Horse trigger a farming boom along the Yakima. Rail service provided access to outside markets and economic incentive to push irrigation still farther into the sage country.

Small irrigation projects undertaken by individuals or groups of farmers were no longer sufficient. In Kittitas County, for example, the Ellensburg Water Company's Town Ditch built in 1885 and the 1889 construction of the West Kittitas Canal supplied water to irrigate 22,000 acres. By 1890 upstart Kittitas County, then only seven years old, quickly had taken the lead in irrigated farming in Washington. That year the county's tally of 25,200 irrigated acres accounted for more than half the state total and was more than 10,000 acres larger than the figure for Yakima County (which then still included most of today's Benton County).

*Early 20th century construction of the Naches-Selah Canal intake structure—backbreaking work by any definition. Yakima Valley Historical Society photo*

The Kittitas lead proved short-lived as equally large enterprises soon got underway in the more spacious Yakima Valley. The Northern Pacific proved to be a primary force. Since the federal government had granted the railroad alternate square-mile sections for a distance of 40 miles on both sides of their transcontinental line west from Lake Superior, the N.P. had become a major land-owner in the Yakima. The checkerboard pattern of railroad land took in about half the valley. Understandably the Northern Pacific was eager to sell property to settlers who were expected to generate traffic for their line.

On this sage frontier, irrigation was a prerequisite to cropping and essential bait for the luring of farmers. With visions of lush green fields and productive agriculturalists reaping bountiful harvests, the Northern Pacific joined with others in 1890 to undertake the most ambitious irrigation scheme to date. Two years later the first 42 miles of the Sunnyside Canal were dedicated at a ceremony befitting a venture planned to eventually irrigate 64,000 acres. The 62-foot-wide aqueduct drew water from a diversion dam and wooden head gates on the Yakima River at Union Gap, and carried it to the newly irrigated north-side lands in the Zillah, Sunnyside, and Grandview areas. More than any other single project, the sizable Sunnyside laid the foundation for the next historic phase in Yakima River irrigation—the entry of the United States government.

By 1903 it was apparent that individuals and even large companies working together had expanded irrigation to its maximum based on diversion of the natural flow of the Yakima and its tributaries. In fact, consecutive, severe late-summer water shortages proved that the 120,000-plus irrigated acres already may have exceeded the capacity of the river to deliver. Clearly what was needed was a comprehensive irrigation system for the entire river basin that would include water storage reservoirs high in the Cascade Mountain headwaters. They could hold back the heavy spring runoff which could be released gradually, permitting an expansion of irrigated acreage and providing more dependable flows.

Convinced that such a colossal enterprise was a job for the federal government, residents of Yakima County petitioned the Secretary of the Interior in January 1903. The previous year passage of the National Reclamation Act had made monies from the sale of federal lands available for development of irrigation projects in the West; the citizens of Yakima County wanted to see some come their way. Surveys showed the project to be feasible and consistent with use of reclamation funds. In 1905 the fledgling Reclamation Service, later the Bureau of Reclamation, embarked upon its ambitious Yakima Project.

The Service began by purchasing the valley's largest private development, the Sunnyside Canal System, and set about planning for its improvement, extension, and expansion of acreage serviced. It was to become merely one element in a grand design that would integrate the water resources of the entire Yakima watershed and more, from its Cascade headwaters to beyond the Yakima River's juncture with the Columbia.

New construction began in 1906 with the monumental Tieton Canal. Although just 12 miles long, this aqueduct west of Yakima would stand as the Reclamation Service's first great construction feat. Its two-plus miles of tunnels through solid rock in the era of horse-drawn machinery, experimental construction techniques, and labor shortages created delays, cost overruns, and fascinating reading in Washington newspapers.

Other elements in the grand scheme were added one by one. Construction activity peaked in the Teens with the addition of landmark structures including Bumping Lake Dam (1910), Kachees Dam (1911), Prosser Canal (1912), and Grandview Canal (1916). Activity shifted north of the Kittitas in the Twenties. The Thirties saw the last major flurry of building with the completion of Cle Elum Dam and Reservoir west of Ellensburg and the

*Yakima Valley propaganda photo by well-known photographer, Asahel Curtis, circa 1910. Yakima Valley Historical Society photo*

large capacity, 90-mile-long Roza Canal System in the Yakima Valley. In the Fifties the Kennewick Division facilities and the Roza power plant provided the finishing touches to a half-century of federal efforts.

Valley petitioners of 1903 were proven correct—the Yakima Project's 462,000 irrigable acres serviced by 6 storage dams, 5 diversion dams, 416 miles of canals, 1,698 miles of lateral, 30 pumping plants and even 2 power plants to help run the system, could not have been accomplished without federal funds.

Entry of the U.S. government into irrigated farming in the Yakima country, and the mere promise of new irrigated land and more assured water supplies was all the ammunition needed by publicists eager to sell their agricultural area to prospective homeseekers. Armed with facts including 300 days of sunshine a year, favored areas with a 200-day freeze-free season, and both a vivid imagination and a flair for turning phrases, boosters set off on one of the Pacific Northwest's most aggressive promotions. Beginning around 1905 and continuing well into the Teens, these ballyhooers perfected their trade. Through booklets, pamphlets, speeches, and every imaginable vehicle they promoted the Yakima Valley with its "most productive soil in the world" and "inexhaustible supply of water." Prospective settlers were told "gold grows on trees here" and "aside from the products of the tropics and subtropics there is practically nothing that can not be produced." Tiny Zillah was "port of call on the sea of prosperity."

Special emphasis was placed on selling valley orcharding even though, at that time, hay crops were the county's largest dollar generator. Apples dominated fruit production and hype with one boomer booklet colored red and cut in the shape of an apple, complete with stem. An early Teens Yakima Commercial Club publication claimed just "ten acres of orchard will support a family in comfort" by producing up to $1,500 an acre profit from apples—this at a time when the average house cost just $1,500!

While waiting the average six to eight years for apple trees to bear commercially, orchardists were encouraged to practice interculture, or the cultivation of other crops between rows of young trees. Potatoes, onions, cabbages, or other vegetables, strawberries, raspberries, melons, or currants, even corn or alfalfa for cow and hog feed, were deemed appropriate. Homeseekers also had the option of purchasing orchard land and then choosing from among several reliable companies to tend young trees until they came of bearing age. Purchasers could be assured income by retaining salaried positions elsewhere while their orchard developed into a profit-making proposition.

All factors, real and exaggerated combined to set off an agricultural boom. The number of Yakima County farms approximately tripled to 5,755 between 1905 and 1920, greatly exceeding today's 4,580 units. New towns sprouted among the green fields and some existing communities doubled and then tripled in size. The Yakima boom continued under its own momentum into the 1930s when number of farms peaked at just over 7,000. Today, with little more than half the record number of farms, Yakima County has a greater on-farm population than all but six of the nation's counties. Its annual $200 million farm earnings rank it number 10, the highest of all non-California counties. Except for some chambers of commerce in California's Central Valley, few question the Yakima Valley's unofficial title of "Fruit Bowl of the Nation."

Strung out astride the Yakima River through Kittitas, Yakima, and Benton counties, the lands served by waters of the Yakima Project are a veritable cornucopia of agricultural products. In an average year some 60 different crops are harvested from fields provided wholly or partially with Project water. In 1982 apples, with a value of close to $120 million, remained firmly established as the dominant crop. Hops were equally entrenched as second ranking with a corresponding $80 million figure. Heavy concentration of both crops in Yakima County ranks it as the nation's largest producer of these two commodities. Cherries, pears, asparagus, grapes, and hay are other major crops synonymous with Yakima country agriculture; in 1982 each produced harvests valued at $20-odd million. Principal among other crops are mint (peppermint and spearmint), wheat, peaches, prunes, plums, corn, potatoes, tomatoes, peppers, melons, and onions.

Livestock continues to be important in the Project, with the 1982 value of cattle marketed second only to apples. Yakima County leads Washington in beef cattle, and neighboring Kittitas County checks in as number three. The Yakima Valley is home base for the last two large sheep range bands, holdovers from an earlier era. Dairying is another important non-cropping type of agriculture, usually ranking as the number-four money generator. Yakima County is the undisputed center of Washington's dairy industry east of the Cascades.

Areas within the Yakima Project claim some of Washington's most diversified and picturesque agricultural landscapes. Project-irrigated farms, with an average of 40 acres of harvested cropland

each, are tiny by Eastern Washington standards. Diminutive farm size and even smaller fields of highly varied crops intensify the land's patchwork quilt fabric. A summer drive south out Lateral A through the Reservation's foliaged Wapato Irrigated District with mist and the scent of mint and apples in the air, or an ascent of Highway 241 north of Sunnyside to look back out over the intricate and lush Roza and Sunnyside districts, make it easy to forget these verdant valleys are climatically near-desert, receiving less than eight or nine inches of precipitation annually. Only the nearby, sharply contrasting bare and brown-toned hills reveal the region's natural thirstiness and emphasize the valley's oasis-like nature.

*Right: Packing Yakima Valley peaches on the J. Van Payton ranch 1900 style. Yakima Valley Historical Society photo*

*Below: Roza Canal above Selah directs precious irrigation water toward the lower valley. John Alwin photo*

Geographically, there are two Yakima Valleys—an Upper and a Lower. North of Union Gap is the higher Upper Valley where elevation of farming districts ranges from 1,000 to over 2,000 feet. A shorter growing season than areas farther downvalley, as low as 120 days in some higher sections west of Yakima, and more sloping land limit crop diversity. Apples dominate in the Naches and Selah, and through the Tieton, West Valley, and Ahtanum. Pears, cherries, and forage round out the major crops in these districts. East of the Yakima the Moxee area is well-known for its heavy hops emphasis.

South of Union Gap in the Lower Valley, irrigated districts vary in elevation from about 1,000 feet down to less than 400 feet. Temperatures average several degrees warmer than in the Upper Valley, and growing seasons lengthen to as long as 200 days. These attributes and more level land make many parts of the Lower Valley particularly suited for row crops. Apples are most widespread, but hops are the most dominant money generator in both the Reservation and Sunnyside Irrigation District. Other Yakima Valley crops run the gamut from numerous varieties of fruits and vegetables, to small grains, mint, forage, and nursery crops.

For many valley families, especially those who participate in the revival of home canning and freezing, trips to the orchards and vegetable fields are a welcome part of the annual routine. Many have their favorite districts and even preferred orchards or stands. Most have a surprising acuity for knowing where certain crops are grown and the timing of various harvests. Yakima city residents eager for the earliest pears know, for example, that harvest in the Prosser area begins up to two weeks before picking starts in the West Valley orchards. Those wanting to buy fresh cantaloupe or corn, peppers, peaches, or plums, know they'll have to head into the Lower Valley.

Elevation alone does not explain locations of all crops. Orchard areas are equally controlled by slope and its orientation. Early spring frosts are the nemesis of orchardists, who gravitate toward areas with minimal frost risks. These are often on hillsides with good cold air drainage, above valley bottoms where potential damaging cold, heavy air tends to settle. Since abundant sunshine promotes better plant growth and sugar development, south slopes are preferred. According to Don Chaplin, Chairman of Yakima County Cooperative Extension, a section just south of Union Gap on the south-facing slopes of Ahtanum and Rattlesnake ridges has especially good cold air drainage and is a prime area for tender, soft fruits.

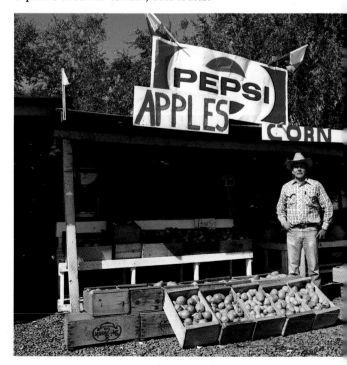

*Left: A razor-edge contact clearly traces the limits of irrigation south of Union Gap. John Alwin photo*

*Right: Viviano R. Ramirez raises 79 acres of vegetables for his own stand. John Alwin photo*

79

*The sticky wine grape harvest in the Yakima is shunned by some seasonal workers. John Alwin photo*

*Keep Out! in English and Spanish. John Alwin photo*

## TAREAS DE CAMPESINOS

Apples and hops, like many of the Yakima Valley's crops, require lots of hand labor, especially at harvest time. This back-breaking work, often stoop labor, involves long days under the hot valley sun. Most residents shun such difficult work, so growers must rely on a corps of local, seasonal farm workers and an army of migrants who move in each harvest season. Hispanics constitute the overwhelming majority of these farm laborers in the Yakima Valley.

The latest Mexican tunes on local radio; conversations in Spanish on the streets of Mabton, Granger, and Sunnyside; colorful local fiestas; and grocery shelves well-stocked with chili peppers and other traditional Mexican foods are reminders of the valley's fast-growing Hispanic population. With more than 25,000, fifteen percent of the county's population, Yakima County has the state's highest percentage of Hispanics. Their presence in the valley in such numbers is linked directly to the area's labor intensive agriculture.

Mexican nationals began arriving legally in large numbers during World War II when farm labor was in short supply. Many stayed on, making the valley their new home. While some older immigrants and their sons and daughters have left the fields, others, out of economic necessity, remain tied to the annual cycle of the crops.

Valley harvests begin with asparagus in early April and run into November and late apples. For some farm laborers winter pruning of grapes and orchard trees may provide additional employment. Field workers are paid either an hourly rate or a set amount for a specific measure. Rates vary with crops and employers. In the mid-Eighties pickers of early peaches received $4 per hour, and $8 for each 900-pound bin of Golden Delicious apples. Wine grape pickers were paid $4 per hour or $8 to $10 for each 400-pound bin. Each crop has its own reputation among field hands. Asparagus harvests are back-breaking and can be cold and wet; wine grapes are considered dirty work with the mess of juice and threat of stings from bees it attracts; cherries are good money and not as delicate as many to pick. Good heavy crops and long days can earn speedy pickers as much as $80 a day.

*Above left: Early peach harvest at the Redman Orchard. Above: Upper Valley on-farm migrant housing provided free of charge. John Alwin photos*

For some locals the entire harvest season is spent in the valley, often with the same farmers and orchardists. Others work in the Yakima for only part of the season and then move on to other Pacific Northwest fruit and vegetable districts.

Bernabe and Mary Trejo and their children are Yakima-based farm workers. Their normal cycle begins working area fields. In early June their children are taken out of school to join in the cherry harvest. All head north to pick cherries later in the month in the Wenatchee district and then in Montana's Flathead Lake area in July. August finds the family back working in the valley. School-aged Trejos are kept out of classes until completion of the apple harvest in early November.

In a recent year the six-member family earned a total of $11,000, "That's not really very much" says Mary. She would like to see all her children receive an education and wants them "out of the field." Mary sees little future in jobs that are, as she says, "going progressively more automated." The cumulative effects of long-term exposure to herbicides and pesticides worries many parents. Fifteen-year-old daughter Angelina, "Cha Cha," doesn't plan on spending her life in the fields. She has her sights on a secretarial career.

Some early 1980s estimates suggest as many as half the Hispanics in Yakima County are undocumented aliens, in the country illegally. This cadre of local illegals and others that move into the valley each spring and summer probably constitutes the majority of the valley's field workers. With local Spanish language radio alerting undocumented aliens through news reports when federal immigration officers set out on one of their several yearly, week-long forays through the valley, apprehensions are frustrated. Even those caught and deported to Mexico have been known to be back in Yakima fields within five days. A well-developed "coyote" system works like a conveyor belt, transporting them back north, sometimes with as many as two dozen jammed into a pickup truck camper.

The general lack of success of the Immigration and Naturalization Service probably pleases most agriculturists who so depend on these hard-working, albeit illegal, Hispanics. Possible new federal legislation to block employment of illegals has Hispanics outraged and Yakima farmers and orchardists worried. Growers believe that without the ability to hire undocumented aliens, crops would rot in the fields.

*Interstate 82 landmark at Selah, a scale in keeping with the productivity of the nation's fruit bowl. John Alwin photo*

Each of the Yakima Valley crops has its own story of early experimentation, acceptance, and diffusion, inevitable ups and downs, and unique aspects of cultivation, harvesting, and marketing. Top-ranking apples and hops have especially long and interesting histories.

From an experimental pioneer planting in the early 1870s, Yakima Valley apple orchards have expanded to 60,000 acres, approximately 8 million trees, and a production of more than a billion pounds of fruit each year. It didn't take long to realize the Yakima country is nearly ideal for production of large, sweet apples. Consistently sunny, warm summer days and a build-up of heat in valleys mean large apples with a high sugar content. Cool nights, especially in fall just before harvest, help finish apples with excellent color and give them extra crispness and longer storage quality. Dry air minimizes disease problems. Fertile, well-drained soils and suitable sloping land are added pluses. Couple these natural advantages with ample water and it isn't surprising that Yakima produces more apples than any other county in the nation.

The Hull family of the Ahtanum has been a part of the Yakima Valley apple industry for five generations. Eighty-four-year-old patriarch, Carroll Hull, says, "I've been dabbling in it ever since I was four years old." Eight decades in the business began as soon as he could stand in the horse-drawn sled and drive it the short distance from tree to tree at harvest time. His father, N.P., is credited with planting one of the region's first commercial orchards in 1896. Characteristic of pioneer efforts, N.P. brought in one or two of every apple variety he could, trying to discover which would perform best. Before irrigation systems were available, he watered his young trees by driving through the eight-acre orchard with a water tank atop a horse-drawn wagon. Water from the newly completed Tieton Canal was a most welcome innovation.

The Arkansas Black, Grimes Golden, and other experimental varieties of Hull's first years as an orchardist are either insignificant or long gone, and the Hull Ranches now grow primarily Red Delicious and Golden Delicious apples. Here and throughout Washington's apple-growing districts Reds are first ranking, followed by Goldens, with

*Left: Two varieties of apples, Golden and Red Delicious, are necessary for cross pollinization in this valley orchard. John Alwin photo*

*Below: Orchardist, Carroll Hull, has been an active member of the Yakima area fruit growing community for eight decades. John Alwin photo*

smaller acreages of Winesaps, Rome Beauties, Jonathons, and several other varieties.

Even though Carroll Hull has witnessed a steady increase in the valley's apple acreage, most recently a 20 percent expansion between 1978 and 1982, he is not optimistic about the future, especially in the Upper Valley. To date the Yakima has defended its share of state apple production, but Hull is convinced it will start slipping as soon as the central Basin's massive new plantings reach bearing age. He doubts the older, established apple areas with their individually small acreages and depleted soil will be able to keep pace.

Orcharding in the senior apple-growing Upper Valley is most threatened. Prior to the 1940s, orchardists controlled worms by spraying with arsenate of lead, some of which remains in the soil to plague today's growers. In no way does it contaminate apples, but it seems to slow tree growth and adds expense to planting, since soil around new trees must be replaced. Because of the problem, some Upper Valley apple ranches have been abandoned and converted to pasture or put to other uses. Suburbanization and urban sprawl onto the picturesque hillsides by outward-expanding Yakima have taken their toll on still more Upper Valley apple acreage.

*Above left: Row upon row of fruit trees grace the gentle slopes of the Upper Yakima Valley. Above: Wind turbines at the Redman Orchard help thwart frost damage by circulating air. John Alwin photos Left: Picking crew at Ahtanum hop yard, circa 1900-1908. Yakima Valley Historical Society photo*

The Yakima Valley's second ranking crop isn't something you look for at fruit and vegetable stands or in supermarket produce bins, but there is a good chance you consume it every time you drink Oly, Rainier, Budweiser, Miller, or other American-label and many foreign beers. Hops, easily the valley's most unique crop, are used as an essential beer-flavoring ingredient—beer without hops is like pretzels without salt.

Bill Harris of Yakima-based Hop Growers of America thinks hops probably first were used in beer hundreds of years ago for reasons other than flavoring. Alpha acid in hops is a natural preservative and when added to beer arrests fermentation and enhances storability. Harris speculates the somewhat bitter taste hops give beer eventually became associated with the brew and was demanded by drinkers who had acquired a taste for the added zip.

Valley hop yards account for about 75 percent of the U.S. production. Each year its output exceeds the production of every nation except beer-loving West Germany. On occasion, of late, the Yakima has even outstripped that of Bavaria's famous Hallertau district.

Driving the valley it isn't always easy for the untrained eye to identify each of the 60 different crops, but there is no doubt with hops. Conspicuous, 18- to 20-foot-tall trellis systems used to support the vines identify the 25,000 acres of hops, this aromatic member of the hemp family, which also includes marijuana.

The fruit, or cone, of this perennial is the hop of commerce. During the late August-through-September harvest, vines are cut by machette-wielding workers driven through the yards on elevated platforms. Hops fresh from the field are stripped of cones, dried in kilns, and compressed like flowers in a book into 200-pound bales. This processing takes place on the hop ranch before shipment to distributors who keep them in cold storage while awaiting brewers' orders. With destinations throughout the nation and world, hops concentrated in the form of pellets vacuum-packed in cellophane bags, and extracts of alpha acid in liquid form are preferred by some distant users.

A long history of production, heavy emphasis on the crop, and the August Hop Festival make the

Moxee area across the river from Yakima synonymous with hops for most area residents. Actually, acreage and production are greater in the Yakima's two other hop growing districts—the Wapato Division (Reservation area) and north of the river in the Sunnyside/Roza Division. With available space in the small Moxee limited, growers have pushed development into the Lower Valley, especially in the Sunnyside/Roza. Over the last six or seven years that Lower Valley area has come to dominate hop production.

Names like Gamache, Brulotte, Charvet, Desmarais, and Perrault on mailboxes in hop districts reflect the dominance of families of French descent in the industry. Contrary to popular misconception, French did not initiate hop growing in the Yakima. Lyman's standard history of the valley

*The big hop vines come down quickly with mechanization. John Alwin photo*

*The Yakima Valley's twenty-foot-tall trellises support the world's second largest hop crop. According to the 1895 edition of the* Encyclopedia Britannica, *when used in medicine, "hops increase the action of the heart, excite the cutaneous circulation and cause diaphoresis...Hops also possess some anaphrodisiac properties...A pillow stuffed with hops forms a well-known domestic remedy for sleeplessness and a bag of hops dipped in hot water is often used as an external application to relieve pain or inflammation, especially of the abdominal organs." John Alwin photo*

credits one Charles Carpenter with raising the first hops in 1872.

The first contingent of French did not arrive in the valley until 25 years later. When Fred Mailloux sent a letter back to his sister in Minnesota in 1896 extolling the farming potential of the Moxee, he set off a mini-migration. That spring his sister, her family, and eight others made the trek west to the new, promising land. In November 1897 an even larger entourage of 57 French Canadians left their Crookston, Minnesota, home to join the others in the Moxee Valley. The French community grew rapidly with the arrival of others from Minnesota and Canada. Initially agriculture centered on general farming and even experimentation with tobacco cultivation. Hops came later. Today 80 to 90 percent of the valley's 150 hop-growing families are of French descent.

*Right: Fruit of the vine, white Riesling. John Alwin photo*

# WINE

## The Hottest Game in Town

It may be a bit premature to move actress Jane Wyman and her Napa Valley wine-making dynasty of prime time soap's "Falcon Crest" to the Yakima Valley, but if present trends continue, a future location change might not be far-fetched. Growing Concord grapes for juice and jelly has a long history in Yakima, Benton, and Franklin counties, but cultivation of *vitis vinifera,* or wine grapes, is something new and is now the hottest game in town.

State wine grape acreage and winery numbers have grown by leaps and bounds. Acreage climbed from just 2,600 in 1979 to more than 8,000 in 1984, with most in the three-county grape-growing area in the Yakima Valley and around the Tri-Cities. Recently, that figure has been expanding at the rate of more than 1,000 acres per year. Likewise, number of Washington wineries ballooned from just three in 1977 to more than 30 by 1984, catapulting the state ahead of New York to position of the nation's second ranking wine-maker. Even if wine acreage reaches 50,000 by the 1990s and eventually exceeds 100,000 acres as some experts predict, Washington still would not overtake number-one California in production. Some think California already has slipped to number-two in quality.

The reputation of wines from Eastern Washington grapes has grown right along with the increasing acreage. A string of best-of-shows, gold, silver, and bronze medals at national and international competitions has helped confirm the region's wine-making status. Numerous factors combine to explain the award-winning nature of these wines. With a latitude approximately that of France's famous Bordeaux and Burgundy regions, the Yakima and low central Basin share a long summer sun. Warm, sunny days allow grapes to ripen with a good sugar-to-acid balance. Cool nights mean grapes are better able to retain important acid, without which they become flat and produce poor wine. Spacious south-facing slopes, especially on the Yakima Folds including the Rattlesnake Hills, Horse Heaven Hills, and the Saddle Mountains' Wahluke Slope, provide excellent exposure. Shallow, well-drained soils are an added plus for grapes. Environmental factors are reflected in the region's tarter and crisper wines, more like those of Europe than California.

Though most Washington wine grape production comes from the Yakima Valley and Tri-Cities region, the Seattle-Puget Sound area claims the greatest concentration of wineries. This is, in part, a reflection of the dominance of Seattle-area investors in the industry and their desire to have as much of the action as close to home as possible. On the east side of the mountains, most wineries have their own associated vineyards. Eastern Washington's gigantic, corporate Chateau Ste. Michelle's Patterson Winery with its adjacent 2,000 acres of grapes, and German-financed Franz Wilhelm Langguth Winery east of Mattawa are atypical. More common are smaller-scale,

family-owned operations or those financed by groups of usually west-side investors.

Quail Run, located five miles north of Zillah on the lower south slope of the Rattlesnake Hills, is one of the newest Eastern Washington wineries. The hillside-perched estate set amidst its well-groomed vineyards would fit right into the Napa Valley countryside. Its 100 acres of premium wine grapes were planted in 1979 and, in wine parlance, Quail Run had its first "crush" three years later.

According to vineyard manager, Kevin Mortensen, Quail Run grows seven varieties of grapes, each carefully matched to slope and one of the vineyard's 10 to 15 soil types. Here, as throughout Eastern Washington, white Riesling is the dominant variety. With wine grapes, quality is paramount to quantity and Mortensen strives to maintain yields at about six tons per acre to help assure the highest quality. With proper management vineyards can remain productive for 50 to 60 years.

Outstanding grapes alone do not guarantee award-winning wine. Just as important is a skilled wine-maker who adroitly can combine science and subjectivity. The proof of Wayne Marcil's skillfulness is already in the bottle. His Quail Run wines have been consistent medal-winners, some in international competition. Wayne has a realistic view of a wine world with its share of nose-in-the-air critics and wine snobs. He admits "You have to play the game," but tries to demystify the fruit of the vine at every opportunity. "I feel very good," he says, "if the general public just comes up to the tasting room and says, 'Boy, I sure like that, that's really good,' and buys a case."

*Far left: Quail Run Vineyards north of Zillah. John Alwin photo*

*Left: Toppenish residents Melva Martinez (r) and her sister, Marisela (l). John Alwin photo*

*Above: Quail Run's wine-maker Wayne Marcil tests sugar content of a white Riesling crush. John Alwin photo*

*Opposite page: Kittitas sweet corn destined for processing in Ellensburg. John Alwin photo*

*Right: Cattle have a long history in the Kittitas Valley. John Alwin photo*

*Below right: Hay and grain dominate the Kittitas agriscape. John Alwin photo*

Though separated by just 30 miles and served by the very same Yakima Project, agriculture in the Kittitas Valley is markedly different than in its sister valley to the south. In the higher Kittitas, cooler climate with its shorter growing season and greater risk of frost is reflected in a less diversified agriculture. Cattle and hay crops, along with wheat, barley, and sweet corn account for most farm income.

At the time of initial white settlement many assumed the valley was too high and cold for cropping. This popular notion was dispelled, however, in 1868 when Frederick Ludi and "Dutch John" Groller moved in and proved vegetables would grow on what is now Ellensburg's south side. Others followed, but from the onset emphasis was on cattle and the production of forage crops. The Kittitas even claims Washington's first registered brand, the bar balloon, still in use by the Schnebly Ranch.

A livestock emphasis has held, and today annual market value of valley cattle equals four times that of all crops combined. No place in Washington is so dominated by cattle and nowhere else in the Evergreen State is the cowboy complex so well-developed. Each Labor Day weekend the Kittitas hosts one of the nation's major rodeos. Year-round, valley residents, on a per capita basis, wear more western belt buckles and cowboy boots than in any other place in the state. People don't look twice here if young intendeds sport cowboy hats in their engagement pictures in the *Ellensburg Daily Record*, or if a candidate for local office poses for campaign posters wearing a Stetson.

The 1982 federal Census of Agriculture showed the county's 78,862 cattle and calves outnumbering residents by better than three to one. Recent years have seen a decline of smaller herds, but an increase in large, 400- to 1,000-head operations. Transhumance, the seasonal movement of livestock from valleys into mountain pastures each summer, remains a colorful local tradition. The annual April cattle drives north into the Blewett Pass area and up to other surrounding highlands attract weekend wranglers and regional reporters eager to capture the flavor of this Old West tradition. With cattle in the high country until the early part of October, or just before start-up of the deer and elk hunting seasons, ranchers traditionally also have had time to be farmers.

An annual precipitation of nine inches on down in this mountain-rimmed basin makes irrigated cropping the norm. The Kittitas is basically hay country, with all varieties combined accounting for just over half the harvested cropland. The area is best known for its timothy, a thoroughbred racehorse hay marketed at tracks from California to New York and overseas, especially in Japan. According to Ron Anderson, president of Ellensburg's Anderson Hay & Grain, the valley is ideally suited to production of outstanding quality timothy. He cites the Kittitas's 1,500 to 2,000 feet elevation and cooler climate as critical. Less heat means a desirable slower growth rate that helps assure a high quality, brightly colored timothy less rank than that produced in warmer climes. The valley's dry summers and infamous winds are actually assets for timothy, allowing the hay, as Anderson says, "to get a nice cure on it," and acquire the fresh smell preferred by finnicky thoroughbreds. Some valley farmers grow a timothy-alfalfa mix, while still others stick to standard alfalfa.

More potato production and expansion of sweet corn acreage in unison with enlargement of Twin City Foods' Ellensburg plant (now the largest processing plant of its kind in the world), have helped diversify valley agriculture, but emphasis remains overwhelmingly on cattle and hay crops. "About all we can do," laments east side farmer Robert Riddle, "is grow hay, grain, sweet corn, and a few

dry peas." The agri-business committee of the local chamber of commerce is looking into new crops, including grass sod and seed, soybeans, sunflowers, garbanzo beans, and even wild rice. A cooler climate than in the adjacent central Basin and Yakima Valley imposes limitations, but perhaps not as many as some locals think. Farmers here talk about a restrictive 90-day frost-free season, but long-term records show a more lengthy average 147 days between the last and first 32-degree frosts.

Frost danger is even more limited on hillsides, which helps explain the growing presence of orchards on the north-facing slope of Manastash Ridge. Valley residents and frequent travellers on the Interstate-82 grade south of Ellensburg have watched this horticultural transformation with interest. Too cool for soft fruit growing, these late-district orchards are almost exclusively in apples and pears. Extra-cool September and early October nights help color both fruits. Apple and pear production remains tiny by Yakima Valley standards, amounting to just 1/300th that of Yakima County, but steady growth should continue. At least one local fruit grower thinks most of the hillside will be in orchards by the end of the century.

Driving the picturesque back roads of the Kittitas another recent trend in rural areas is even more apparent. Horse enthusiasts have discovered the valley. Their tidy landscapes with miles of newly painted fences, lush pastures, and ample stables make some sections look like they belong outside Lexington, Kentucky.

Some locals estimate there are 11,000 horses in the Kittitas and that number increases each year. Local Gaylord Bruketta has been involved with valley thoroughbreds for a decade and is convinced that "within 10 years there'll be more horses here, both show and thoroughbred, than cattle 20 years ago." In the mid-Sixties there were 72,000 head of cattle in the county!

Numerous factors explain the influx. The area's equine passion has been one major draw. The Kittitas may be Washington's most horse-conscious community, an ideal setting for professional horse breeders and racers. The valley's somewhat cooler climate and high-grade hay are additional lures. For racehorse owners the central location between Washington's three major tracks in Seattle, Yakima, and Spokane is a practical consideration. Locals may be aghast at the $3,000 per acre price for land, but Seattle-area buyers feel almost guilty paying such prices.

Opposite page: Down from their summer pasture in Blewett Pass country, these sheep kick up the dust on the old Vantage Highway to grazing in the stubble fields outside Ellensburg. John Alwin photo

Above: Cutting hay in the Kittitas.

Above right: Horse enthusiasts have discovered the valley.

Bottom right: A thick cloud of smoke billows from burning stubble.

Right: On the Robert Riddle farm. John Alwin photos

# COLUMBIA BASIN PROJECT

Of all Eastern Washington's component regions, the central Basin section was deemed least promising for agriculture. Early white visitors were amazed at its bleak, sterile, and in some places, desert-like surfaces of shifting sand dunes. Through much of the 19th century, first explorers, and then others traversing or even skirting this dry heart of Eastern Washington, consistently described it in less-than-glowing terms. Outsiders saw it as "ugly desert," "hot, dry, desolate waste," "the most disgusting country," "dismally barren," "parched like a cinder," and "little else than miserable desert." It even was compared to the infamous Sahara and the scorching deserts of Arabia. The Basin's parched center almost solely was responsible for the 19th century notion of a Great Columbia Desert.

As long as the higher, wetter, and more agriculturally desirable districts on the Basin's flanks were available to settlers, it was understandable that the dry center remained largely the domain of cattlemen and roving bands of range sheep. The region's first appreciable influx of settlers at the turn of the century was more the result of a push out of filled adjacent farming districts than the pull of these thirsty lands. Only after agrarian settlement approached capacity in the surrounding Palouse, Walla Walla, Big Bend, and other sections did the farming frontier push down into the long-avoided central Basin.

The dates of appearance of Basin towns reflect the region's relatively late coming of age—Ephrata platted in 1901; Quincy laid out in 1902; Othello incorporated in 1910; and Neppel (later renamed Moses Lake) founded in 1910.

*Irrigation water has transformed thirsty Quincy Basin into a verdant garden. John Alwin photo*

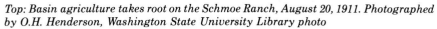

*Top: Basin agriculture takes root on the Schmoe Ranch, August 20, 1911. Photographed by O.H. Henderson, Washington State University Library photo*

*Bottom: Eliminating the competition, a big jack-rabbit hunt, December 5, 1912. Photographed by O.H. Henderson, Washington State University Library photo*

*Top: Quincy, view from water tank, June 11, 1911. Photographed by O.H. Henderson, Washington State University Library photo*

*Bottom: The first step, a far-sighted farmer breaks virgin ground in the southern part of the Basin. 1909 Asahel Curtis photograph, Washington State Historical Society*

Optimism and prosperity grew in the first decade of the new century as homeseekers moved in to claim their piece of one of the West's last frontiers. Provided area drylanders received at least average precipitation annually along with a suitable seasonal distribution, acceptable wheat yields were possible, at least for awhile on the freshly broken ground. In 1910 newly created Grant County, which includes much (2,660 square miles) of the low central Basin, already boasted 1,607 farms and 180,000 acres of wheat.

Eighty-two-year-old Jake Melcher was born and raised on the central Basin's homesteading frontier. His mother and father, Henry and Katie, had immigrated from Germany to Russia prior to their arrival in Portland, Oregon, in 1899. It didn't take long before encouragement of friends already in the area lured the Melchers north to the rapidly filling sage country 20 miles southwest of Odessa. As a young boy, Jake remembers his dad grubbing off brush with a sulky and broke, local wild horses. With timber in short supply in this treeless country, sage, he recalls, was an important source of fuel for the family's large tin stove. For Jake's family and other sagebrushers, a farming life in the basin looked promising.

For central Basin farming families the euphoria that had accompanied the rapid influx of population and expansion of wheatlands during the century's first decade was not repeated in the Teens. In this marginal rainfall country even modest shortfalls of precipitation or slight shifts in the seasonal pattern made the difference between good crops and no crops. Settlers conditioned to farming in better-watered districts learned the hard way that the lower the average annual precipitation, the greater the year to year variation. Vicissitudes of weather, problems with weed control, declining yields, and severe wind erosion of the area's light sandy soil showed that many quarters were ill-suited to dryland wheat farming. The drylander had pushed too far, and even in more suitable areas had oversettled.

The early Teens marked the beginning of a difficult period of decline and agricultural readjustment. One by one farms folded, neighbors moved on, and sage and cheat moved in to fill many of the abandoned fields. Dry farming failures stimulated interest in irrigation, but no major action was taken on that front for another generation. By 1920 the number of Grant County farms had dropped to 1,110 and wheat acreage contracted proportionally.

Farm population and dryland acreage continued their decline in the Twenties. By 1924 Grant County wheat acreage was down to less than half the 1910 figure. Rather than improve, conditions grew even more impossible in the late-Twenties as the double whammy of Washington's worst drought of record and the ensuing Depression knocked the bottom out from the region's already precarious agricultural economy.

First came drought, brutal, persistent, and devastating. The earliest signs of trouble appeared in the spring of '28 when days stretched into weeks and then months with hardly a sprinkle. In the eight-month period from May to December that year, precipitation totaled just 2-1/2 inches at Ephrata and less than 3 inches at Quincy. The drought intensified the next year when just 3.15 inches fell at Ephrata, 3.49 at Quincy, and 4.09 on Odessa. Rain gauges on the Wahluke Slope failed to register even 3 inches. The entire central Basin remained firmly in the grip of the merciless drought through 1930 as more than one farmer pondered the area's earlier comparisons with the Sahara.

Stripped of their natural protective vegetative cover and too dry to grow crops, the region's desiccated, sandy soils were laid bare and susceptible to Dust Bowl-like wind erosion. Even though then just a young girl, Garnita Foster Schell vividly remembers the terrible dust storms her family experienced in '29 and '30 at their farm north of Ruff. She can still visualize the wind-whipped sand dunes that repeatedly buried fences and the cloth tied around one's face when venturing outside. "You couldn't even get away from the dust inside," she remembers, "we'd pile all the furniture in the middle of the floor and cover it with sheets and blankets."

Severe and protacted drought alone would have been enough to prompt wholesale abandonment of central Basin farming areas. The dovetailing Depression merely amplified the exodus. Dry years meant total crop failures, or at best two or three bushels per acre that might be grazed off by livestock. The Depression meant lack of markets, low prices, and unavailability of capital. By the hundreds, once hopeful farmers simultaneously were pushed off the land and out of the region by impossible weather and economics, and were pulled away by the hope of employment both near and far.

By 1930 Grant County's 1920 complement of 1,110 farms had plummeted to 787 and continued its slide to just 600 in 1940. Today, abandoned and weather-worn farmsteads in the central Basin and surrounding dryland farming districts are visual reminders of those whose dreams of prosperity on the Eastern Washington steppe were dashed.

Large-scale irrigated agriculture was on the way in the Thirties, but for many it would arrive too late. Proposals for irrigation of the central Basin have a surprisingly long history. By the late 19th century projects in the equally dry Yakima Valley, as well as in the Kittitas and Wenatchee valleys, had proven the attributes of irrigated farming in marginal rainfall areas. Time and time again as drylanders watched their wheat fields wilt and wither under drought conditions, their farming counterparts in the valleys to the west harvested bumper crops of fruit and forage crops. In the 1890s proposals for irrigating large sections of the central Basin began surfacing.

Various Basin irrigation proposals came and went between 1892 and the fateful year of 1918 when Eastern Washington residents were thrust into a heated, fifteen-year-long battle between proponents of two equally ambitious schemes. One camp was centered in Ephrata and rallied around local attorney, Billy Clapp's not totally new proposal for a Grand Coulee Dam and the pumping of water out of the reservoir and into Grand Coulee. Rufus Woods, the fiery publisher of *The Wenatchee World,* was an exceptionally vocal member. His newspaper became the group's most effective propaganda vehicle. The opposition group was Spokane-based. Their equally grand plan called for construction of a gravity-waterway system of canals and natural drainage routes to divert water about 130 miles from Albeni Falls on north Idaho's Pend Oreille River to a storage reservoir near Ritzville.

It was the Grand Coulee Dam advocates versus the Gravity Plan proponents, the sagebrushers versus the city slickers, the pumpers versus the ditchers. Both groups claimed their project would irrigate two to two-and-a-half million acres of arid and semiarid Basin lands, but that was as far as the agreement went. Each hired experts to reinforce their claims and denounce those of the opposition. Coercion, half-truths, and just plain shenanigans found their way into the donnybrook, the likes of which Eastern Washingtonians have yet to see again.

History and the 550-foot-tall Grand Coulee Dam record which group prevailed. In July 1933, $63 million was allocated by the Federal Administration of Public Works for construction of a Grand Coulee Dam. The undertaking was a natural for President Roosevelt who spoke in person of the project's power, farming, and job benefits at the August 1934 dam site dedication.

Roosevelt's promise of thousands of new jobs was soon filled, the power and farm benefits followed. By the summer of 1937 8,000 people were employed in the immense construction project. It is still easy to find Eastern Washington residents in their late sixties to early eighties who are eager to share recollections of their construction days on the big dam. They are happy to talk about the coffer dams, shaping bedrock, huge concrete buckets, and the temporary construction towns of Mason City and Government Town, but usually shy away from detailed discussions of goings on along Grand Coulee's infamous boom town B Street with its 24-hour-a-day opportunities for manly forms of rest and relaxation.

Though Grand Coulee was designed primarily as an irrigation dam, the outbreak of World War II near its completion date meant a temporary shift of emphasis to power production. Generators were rushed to the dam site and soon were producing the electricity essential to the Pacific Northwest's very substantial contribution to the nation's war effort.

Following World War II emphasis at Grand Coulee shifted back to irrigation and the Columbia Basin Project of which it was the keystone. Major pumping plants, reservoirs, and hundreds of miles of canals and laterals were put in place in the Forties. Finally, on August 10, 1951, 18 years after the

*The big dam takes shape, June 3, 1937. U.S. Bureau of Reclamation photo*

initial site preparation for Grand Coulee Dam had commenced, the first test water moved out of the reservoir behind the dam and into the system. Each year between 1951 and 1958, irrigation water became available to 50,000 to 65,000 acres with that rate dropping in subsequent years. Finally, the irrigators' long wait was over and the agrarian metamorphosis of the central Basin was underway.

Gigantic 550-foot-tall, 5,225-foot-long Grand Coulee Dam, the largest concrete structure in the world, plugs the Columbia and impounds 151-mile-long Franklin D. Roosevelt Lake. Even this towering dam isn't high enough to raise the reservoir level to the top of the river canyon. This feat is accomplished by some of the world's largest pumps. They draw water up the remaining 280 feet and over the rim through six elephantine tubes and send it on its way to the Project's 2,200 farms and 50,000-plus irrigated acres.

Once over the canyon rim irrigation water is directed into Banks Lake equalizing reservoir. This

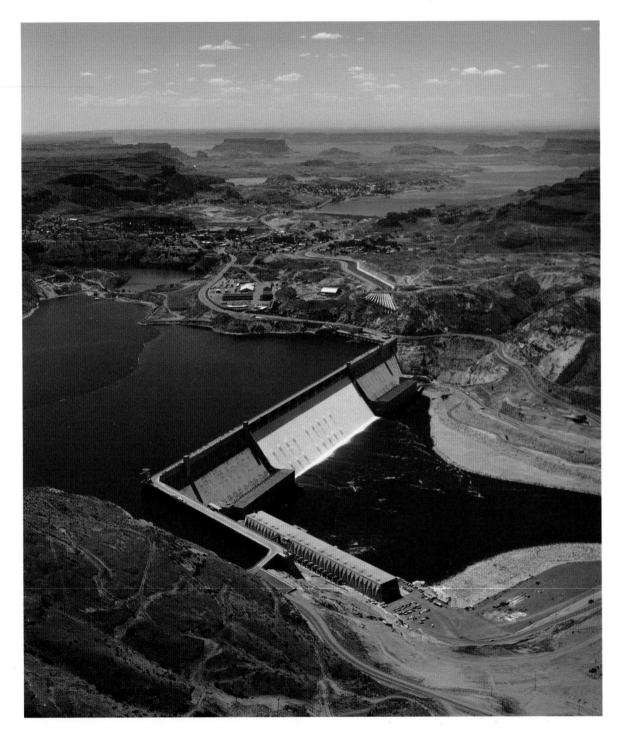

*Left: Grand Coulee Dam and north end of Banks Lake equalizing reservoir in the Grand Coulee. New third power plant in foreground. Town of Grand Coulee, left center, and Electric City in distance. Steamboat Rock visible near horizon. U.S. Bureau of Reclamation photo*

27-mile-long lake was formed by damming both the north and south ends of nature's already beautifully excavated Upper Grand Coulee. From Banks Lake water is released into the Main Canal through south end Dry Falls Dam and conveyed southward, enroute passing through a 1,000-foot-long siphon and almost two-mile-long Bacon Tunnel. Farther along water plunges over 165-foot-tall Summer Falls, a vestige of the Scabland Floods, and into Billy Clapp Lake. Below this reservoir the Main Canal splits. Some water is diverted into the 87-mile-long East Low Canal which waters the Project's eastern section. The remainder flows into 88-mile-long West Canal. All totaled the Project's life-giving circulation system includes an interconnected network of 333 miles of main canals, 1,959 miles of laterals, and 2,761 miles of drains and wasteways.

Agricultural land in the immense Columbia Basin Project reaches from Soap Lake on the north 90 miles south to beyond the mouth of the Snake. These are among Washington's and the nation's most productive farm lands. The area's sandy soils are surprisingly well-suited to cropping. A long freeze-free season (210 days for the Wahluke Slope on the south flank of the Saddle Mountains), abundant sunshine, and warm to hot growing season temperatures are regional hallmarks. Combine these attributes with relatively inexpensive water liberally applied at 40 to 60 inches annually and you have the prerequisite of yet another Eastern Washington agricultural cornucopia. Grant County, which includes most of the Project acreage, annually produces scores of different crops and ranks in the top 35 nationally for average farm earnings, second only to Yakima County in the entire Pacific Northwest.

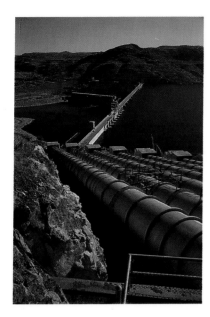

*Above: Giant siphon tubes draw water 280 feet out of Franklin Roosevelt Lake and direct it to the Project's farmlands. Bureau of Reclamation photo*

*Right: Columbia Basin Project, Bureau of Reclamation map.*

Project statistics for a recent year clearly show its agricultural credentials. In 1982 the Project's 2,200 farms and their 521,400 irrigated acres produced 56 different crops with a gross value of $289 million. Five or six major commodities dominate. Potatoes, late and early varieties combined, ranked first in dollar value with 25 percent, even though grown on just 40,200 acres, or less than 8 percent of the irrigated acreage. Other top crops in order of rank and corresponding acreage that year were: alfalfa hay at 16 percent (112,000 acres), wheat with 15 percent (122,700 acres), feed grain corn at 7 percent (53,900 acres), and sweet corn with 5 percent (18,400 acres). The remaining 32 percent of total crop value came from a wide range of crops including apples, asparagus, dry beans, grapes, onions, and numerous varieties of seeds (peas, alfalfa, carrots, clover, radishes, corn, onions, and beans). The 200,000-plus head of cattle finished annually in feedlots and the additional thousands raised on Project farms rank livestock as a major non-crop dollar generator.

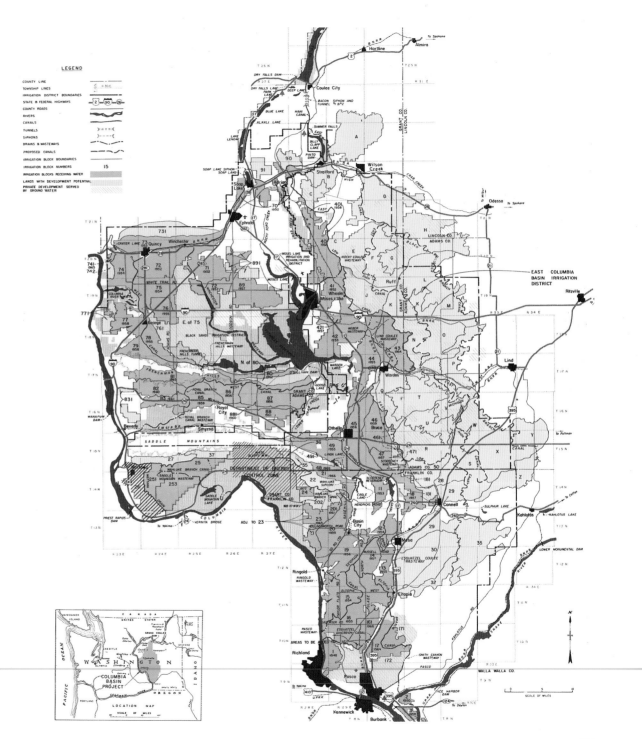

## A desert, pure and simple

The succession of negative perceptions of the dry central Basin continued into the late 1800s. In August 1879, Lieutenant Thomas W. Symons travelled through the region on a trying expedition from Walla Walla to Fort Okanogan at the mouth of the river of the same name. His account of the leg of the journey between the White Bluffs on the Columbia north to the area east of Moses Lake sounds more like a trek across the desert wastes of the Sahara than Eastern Washington.

*"Proceeding somewhat to the northeast, to skirt Saddle Mountain, we soon found ourselves getting into a country more sandy and more rolling, and our mules and horses had greater difficulty in getting along. In the afternoon, being on the lookout for water, we made for a green-looking spot off to the east, hoping it was a spring. In this we were disappointed, and we continued on our way until nine o'clock at night, when, not finding any water, we unloaded and made ourselves as comfortable as possible without it. The next morning before daylight we took up our laborsome march through the sands of the desert and traveled until about two in the afternoon, when, as our animals were suffering intensely from thirst, and as we were uncertain about what lay before us directly north, we concluded to strike to the westward, as from all the indications it was more likely to give us a supply of water. About three o'clock we came to an old road, which gave indications of having at one time been well traveled, and we turned and followed it to the northward, trusting that it would take us to water.*

*A desert, pure and simple. John Alwin photo*

*At five o'clock our animals seemed utterly unable to carry their packs any further, and so we unloaded them and piled up our baggage and kept on without it. About nine o'clock that night we came to a small alkali pond, which, vile as it was, seemed like nectar to us and to our poor horses and mules.*

*The country we had traveled was covered partly with sage-brush, bunch-grass, and weeds, and was utterly waterless and lifeless. Not even the cheerful coyote lived there, for not one lulled us to sleep or molested our abandoned provisions and camp equipage."*

Quoted in Thomas W. Symons, *Report on An Examination of the Upper Columbia River and the Territory in its Vicinity* (1882), p. 122.

Potatoes, alfalfa hay, and wheat have been top ranking since the early 1950s, but other former leading crops either have fallen in rank or disappeared. In 1954, for example, dry beans produced the highest valued crop, but by 1982 barely made it into the top ten. By the early 1960s sugar beets consistently ranked as the number one crop, but all production ceased following the 1970s closure of the U & I sugar refinery at Moses Lake.

More recently, acreage of corn, grapes, and apples has grown dramatically. Expansion of sweet corn acreage has been especially noticeable, doubling since the late 1970s. Basin sweet corn is highly regarded by processors who use it in almost 100 brands marketed nationally. Regular fall travellers on I-90 west of Moses Lake are familiar with the steady stream of semi-trucks hauling single and tandem hopper trailers overflowing with ears of corn, straining up the steep grade west of Vantage enroute to processing plants in Ellensburg and several Western Washington communities.

Project grape acreage has grown with interest in wine grapes regionwide, but still accounts for little more than one percent of total crop value. "It's a loud crop. There's a lot more noise about those grapes than acres," says Les Gius, who owns a 60-acre Red Delicious orchard west of Quincy. "In comparison to apples, the wine grapes are peanuts," he says. Statistics back this up and reveal a Basin apple boom that is remaking the landscape on thousands of acres in the western section of Grant County.

The central Basin's apple growing prowess shouldn't surprise anyone according to one local orchardist who says, "If Yakima can grow good apples and Wenatchee can grow good apples, there's no reason why we in between can't do the same." Not only does western Grant County share some of the apple growing attributes of its rivals to the south and north, it has some important advantages. Spacious, gently sloping land with suitable soils and adequate frost-free season cover tens of thousands of acres.

*Circles on the plains, the new geometry of center pivot irrigation. U.S. Bureau of Reclamation photo*

*The drone of crop dusting planes overhead is part of a Columbia Basin summer. U.S. Bureau of Reclamation*

*Left: Boom-crop blossom season, apples in the Basin. Above left: Emilio Mendoza bags Red Delicious. Above right: Randy Ferguson, Quincy area crop duster prefers the time-proven Grumman AgCat. John Alwin photos*

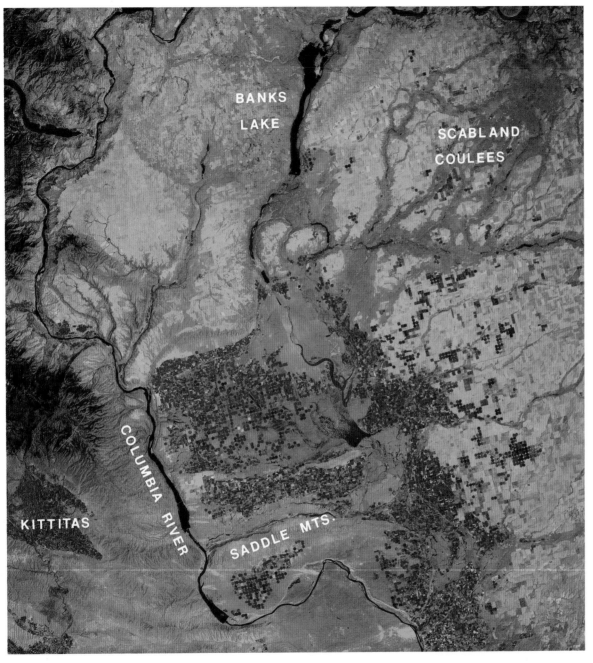

A view from space on July 18, 1979. Landsat image of the central Basin and adjacent areas, taken from an altitude of 570 miles. Approximately 115 by 115 miles square. False color, such that lush vegetation, including irrigated crops, register as intense red. Note numerous circles of center pivot irrigation. From U.S. Geological Survey, EROS Data Center.

The Yakima and Wenatchee districts "don't have the land we do," says orchardist Gius. Here plantings tend to be larger and more economic than the "little, tiny orchards" on the Cascade's east slope. One new orchard on the west end of the Wahluke Slope blankets almost 2,000 acres and another nearby planting on line for 1985 will cover 1,000 acres.

In addition to having larger and more economical orchards, central Basin apple growers are spared the lead arsenate contaminates of their old-orchard counterparts. Many plantings of usually semi-dwarf trees at 300 to 600 trees per acre is yet another economic plus for central Basin orchardists.

As Horticultural Extension Agent for Grant-Adams counties, Ray Hunter has been involved with area apple production for 21 years. "When I started, Grant County had 1,600 acres of apples. Today apple acreage is *conservatively* put at 21,500." Others suggest a figure of at least 25,000 acres. All agree that the county is now second only to Yakima County in apple acreage and that figure climbs dramatically each year. Hunter estimates that only about half the county's acreage is of bearing age, testimony to the recent boom since it takes five to six years for apple trees to reach commercial production.

Locals and outside investors have discovered the tax advantages and potential profits of area apple orchards. Some plantings are developed by large groups of investors sometimes including overseas capital, with each individual owning perhaps as little as five acres.

Hunter estimates he receives a minimum of 200 inquiries a year from farmers and investors interested in developing orchard property. He has written a guide for prospective orchardists. Hunter directs people to suitable sloped land with a minimum of 165 frost-free days. He steers them away from areas with calcareous or highly alkaline soils. The Priest Rapids-Mattawa area has been especially popular of late, and now has 11,400 acres in apples of which, according to Hunter, no more than 1,000 acres were of bearing age in 1984.

Experts agree the central Basin still has at least 50,000 acres suitable for apple orchards, much in the Wahluke and Royal slope areas. If that area were developed, Grant County would surpass Yakima County, which now ranks as the nation's top apple producer. Western Grant County could become the country's largest apple producing region. Or, if expanded markets are not found for all new production, it might be an excellent place to collect firewood in 15 or 20 years.

*Ephrata's enterprising Lewis Williams, backyard horticulturalist, mans his stand. John Alwin photo*

*Lining WB48E on the Wahluke Slope, August, 1983. John Alwin photo*

As of the mid-1980s water from the Columbia Basin Project served just 541,000 of an originally authorized 1,095,000 acres. Most of the area still unserved by federal water is in the large East High, a swath of territory in the Project's eastern section. Large portions are served by private deep well irrigation and even more is in dryland grain production.

Completion of the Project and delivery of water to the approximately 385,000 East High acres is controversial. Many drylanders want nothing to do with irrigated farming, while others operating expensive 400- to 600-foot-deep wells are eager for a cheaper alternative. With a projected cost of $1.6 billion, who pays what, when, remains an overriding factor.

Some argue that expanding agricultural acreage and harvests at a time of overproduction and depressed prices makes little sense. Others counter by suggesting it is mostly dryland crops that are in surplus and the greater cropping options under irrigation would mitigate against aggravating market surpluses. Environmentalists and power interests worry about the loss of in-stream flows in the Columbia. Proponents weigh such costs against the hope of an agricultural renaissance with growth of population and industry similar to the first decade of the Project, when each 10,000 acres of newly irrigated land meant 1,022 more people in area farms and towns.

In this era of reduced government interest in large public works projects, plans to complete the East High persist. A second Basin Siphon and Tunnel next to the originals south of Coulee City have been completed and, according to Dale Olson, Chief of the Columbia Basin Project's Realty and Repayment Branch, capacity to serve the new acreage is already in place above that point. The only requirements are modification of the Main Canal north of Summer Falls, a bifurcation there, and construction of the East High and Black Rock Branch canals and associated laterals. In the summer of 1984 the Bureau of Reclamation was about to let a contract for an environmental assessment of the completion of the Columbia Basin Project. By the late '80s we will know if funds for development will be forthcoming and a doubling of federally irrigated Project acreage will finally become a reality.

*A hard-working Hispanic on the Paradise Flats outside Othello. John Alwin photo*

*John Alwin photo*

# BIG BEND

The Big Bend of the Columbia River lends its name to Eastern Washington's most extensive agricultural region. This 7,000-square-mile, arc-shaped farming district takes in all or part of six counties immediately east and north of the Columbia Basin Project's developed section. Included are Whitman County west of the Palouse, most of Adams, the extreme southwest corner of Spokane, virtually all of Lincoln, northern Grant, and most of Douglas.

Panoramic vistas of golden grainlands, dust devils swirling across bare fallowed fields that often extend right up to the front door of farmhouses, and struggling small towns with their obligatory complement of rail-side elevators are ubiquitous in this farming district. The Big Bend is wheat country. This is reflected everywhere, from a Waterville restaurant's "Combine Room" and the local "Shocker" high school sports teams, to Ritzville, home of the 3500-member Washington Association of Wheat Growers and the annual Wheat Lands Communities' Fair. Region wide, wheat is grown on more than a million acres with Lincoln and neighboring Adams ranking number two and three in Washington and as two of the nation's major wheat producing counties. In an average year the Big Bend's harvest exceeds that of its more famous neighbor, the Palouse, by at least 30 percent.

Except in the parched western section of Adams County where deep wells provide water for irrigated farming, much under center pivot, Big Bend remains a dominantly non-irrigated district. Since 1915 Washington State University's Dry Land Research Unit southwest of Ritzville has helped farmers refine agriculture in the Big Bend's driest inner arc. There, a two-year crop rotation of

*It's almost like mining at Ritzville as front-end loaders move grain about in readiness for shipping. John Alwin photo*

*Above left: B & S Feedlot fattens cattle for market. Above right: Last summer's bounty sits unclaimed at Ritzville as a new crop of winter wheat takes hold. Lower right: Quick removal of wheat stubble north of Wilbur. Lower left: Dean's Drive-In, Reardon. John Alwin photos*

*Above left: Visiting Ritzville takes on Kahlotus in soccer. Above right: A weather-worn relic from another time, east of Waterville. Lower right: Hooper's nerve center. John Alwin photos*

wheat:fallow remains common. In the region's topographically higher and wetter peripheral sections, farmers increasingly are moving toward a three-year, wheat:barley:fallow sequence and even continuous cropping where moisture conditions permit. Although cash grain farming dominates, some operators also run cattle. Most would be classified as cow-calf operations, producing young animals for shipment to feedlots both within the region and as far afield as the Midwest Corn Belt.

Since the Big Bend's historic homestead peak, the fabric of agrarian occupance has thinned in each successive decade. A coarser fabric of 2,000-plus-acre grain farms has replaced the quarter and half section units of the area's original farmers. Unlike within irrigated districts where abandoned farmhouses and outbuildings usually are

removed promptly to allow for a few more acres of precious ground, these weather worn relics of earlier times are not uncommon in this dominantly dryland farming country.

Farm consolidation has meant rural depopulation and difficult times for many of the region's small farm-supply and grain-handling communities. In the era of more densely populated hinterlands and horse-drawn grain wagons, a close spacing of towns was essential. Today, a reduced rural populace means fewer customers for local business communities, and modern transportation brings larger and more distant towns within easy reach. Why drive five miles into Ralston when the bright lights of Ritzville are only 10 miles farther? Recent rail abandonments and growing popularity of multi-car, unit grain trains available only at larger terminals have added to small town woes.

# EASTERN WASHINGTON'S HUTTERITES

Next time you sit down to enjoy cole slaw at the Colonel's in Moses Lake, Odessa, Quincy, or Othello, or pour your Spokane-bottled Darigold milk, there's a chance you are consuming products from some of the Big Bend's most efficient farmers. They are Hutterites, members of a distinctive communal religious group that has been at home on the area's steppe lands for a quarter century.

The Hutterite religion began in Europe at the time of the Protestant Reformation about 400 years ago. Like the related Old Order Amish and Mennonite groups, Hutterites refused membership in a state religion, rejected infant baptism, and were pacifists. These beliefs alone would have been enough to set them apart from mainstream religions of the time, their insistence on communal ownership of property and colony lifestyle merely widened the rift. Persecution followed them as they shifted from place to place in search of safe refuge between their 1528 founding in today's Austria/Czechoslovakia and their 1780s arrival in Russia.

Between 1874 and 1877 approximately 800 immigrated to what became South Dakota. About half broke from communal life and the remainder were organized into three colonies, or *Bruderhofs*. Today, each of the three different Hutterite sects—Dariusleut, Lehrerleut, and Schmiedeleut—can trace their origin to one of these original colonies.

Hutterites moved west into the semiarid Columbia Basin in the mid-Fifties, farming a leased unit near Moses Lake. By 1960 excessive land rental and a desire for a somewhat better-watered area led the group 18 miles west of Spokane where they established Espanola Colony, Eastern Washing-

*Espanola Colony, Eastern Washington's first.*

*Wash day at Marlin Colony. John Alwin photos*

ton's first. Three other full-fledged Dariusleut colonies followed: Warden Colony outside the city of the same name in 1973; Marlin Colony north of Ruff in 1975; and Stahlville Colony northwest of Ritzville in 1980. Two much smaller groups of Hutterites, one from Montana and the other out of Alberta, are attempting to form additional colonies east and southeast of Odessa.

Efficiency, productivity, and large profits are a prerequisite to perpetuation of Hutterite culture. With a birth rate still up to four times the national figure, each *Bruderhof* must prepare for its own daughter colony. Once a colony's population exceeds much over 110 it usually divides in two. Half the group remains in the parent colony and the rest move on to the new daughter colony.

For Hutterites the *Bruderhof* not only provides the economic means for life, it also affords safe refuge from an outside world they view as filled with sin and temptation. A prohibition on radios and televisions helps keep evil influences out. Only by living within the *Bruderhof,* they feel, can they maintain God's order and receive eternal life.

Although Hutterites resist full integration into the dominant American culture, they

are not hermits. Colony members interact within their regional farming community and welcome occasional outside visitors.

Demographics suggest more Eastern Washington colonies in the future. Even though Hutterite families now average "just" five or six children, that still means rapid population growth and inevitable daughter colonies. Espanola already has formed its first daughter colony (Warden) within the region. Hutterites frequently travel back and forth between colonies visiting family. Understandably, remoteness from the main concentration of their brethren in the northern Great Plains has worked to limit formation of daughter colonies in the distant Columbia Basin.

Jacob Gross, minister of the Marlin Colony, is pleased with what he feels is his colony's "good relationship with locals." Reverend Gross admits "We're a very peculiar people. According to our beliefs we're what they call communists, but not the Red." Any friction with neighbors he attributes to that philosophical difference and the fact that Hutterites are so efficient they don't have to rely on outside labor. At least a little misunderstanding of this nonconformist group by locals has been a part of Hutterian life for over 400 years.

# WENATCHEE FRUIT DISTRICT

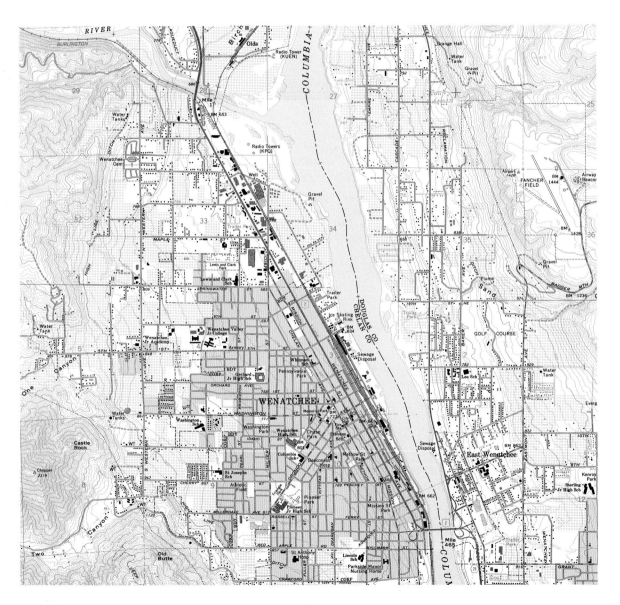

From Wenatchee to Entiat, Chelan, and north to Brewster, an orderly progression of row upon row of fruit trees blankets the narrow valley bottoms of the Columbia and its major west side tributaries. Cavernous packing sheds and cold storage facilities are common sights, as are apple-prefix business names and the annual summer influx of pickers. This is the Wenatchee Fruit District, one of the Pacific Northwest's premier tree fruit regions.

The Wenatchee is part of an international Wenatchee-Okanogan Fruit Belt that stretches from south of the city, up the Columbia and north up the Okanogan Valley into British Columbia's southern interior. In our Eastern Washington region most orchards are concentrated within a one- to two-mile-wide belt on either side of the Columbia in Chelan and Douglas counties. Horticultural stringers carry orchards out of the Basin and into the adjacent mountains along the Wenatchee and Entiat rivers and into the Lake Chelan lowland.

To the north in the cooler Okanogan County section, production is overwhelmingly apples, with that fruit accounting for over 90 percent of orchard acreage. Apples dominate in the Chelan and Douglas section, but large acreages of pears and cherries and smaller plantings of peaches, apricots, and nectarines add to this area's fruit basket reputation.

As in the rival apple growing Yakima Valley and the upstart central Basin, soil, topography, and climate and abundant irrigation water translate into world-class apples. Fertile and well-drained soils, suitable sloping land, dry air, long summer days, cool nights, and copious amounts of water drawn from adjacent Cascade mountain streams and the Columbia River, make this an

*Section of the Wenatchee topographic quadrangle. Orchards are shown by green dot symbol. Small black squares represent homes in non-urban areas.*

*South of Chelan along the Columbia. John Alwin photo*

apple producing rival to the number one ranking Yakima. The Yakima Valley apple harvest may be equal to that of the Wenatchee-Okanogan, but less crop diversity in the more northerly of Eastern Washington's two major fruit districts makes the Wenatchee a much more apple-conscious area. It is home to the Washington State Apple Commission, which works diligently to assure high standards and develop markets for the two billion pounds of fresh apples marketed annually.

Washington has been the foremost supplier of apples to the nation each year except one since the early 1920s. Three-fourths of state apples are consumed as "fresh" fruit, with the remainder processed into juice, cider, applesauce, and other apple by-products within the apple growing district and marketed nationally under labels including Tree Top and Seneca.

In the 1950s a revolutionary new storage process called Controlled Atmosphere (CA) arrived in Eastern Washington's apple districts. CA involves storage of the fruit in a nitrogen-rich, air tight cold room in which oxygen is held at a low 2.5 percent and carbon dioxide is kept under one percent. This carefully controlled environment retards the ripening process and, according to experts, maintains apples in the same condition as when they were picked. CA has broadened the market season from six to 12 months. When marketed, usually starting in January and running into July, these crisp and juicy apples command top prices. Approximately 60 percent of Washington's crop are now CA apples.

Most of Washington's fresh apple crop is consumed domestically, the majority transported to distant markets via refrigerated trucks. California ranks as the number one customer, followed by Texas, New York, and Illinois, in that order. Los Angeles, New York, Chicago, and San Francisco are the top four customer cities. The Commission keeps careful tabs on shipments to hundreds of cities. They can report, for example, that the Los Angeles area received 3,426,000 42-pound boxes in the 1981-82 marketing season, while Paducah, Kentucky, received 18,000 boxes; Texarkana, Texas, 1,100 boxes; and Devil's Lake, North Dakota, 1,000 boxes.

Eastern Washington's fresh apple crop of approximately 50,000,000 boxes is expected to rise to 80,000,000 in just a few years. Marketing of the growing harvest has involved the Apple Commission in an aggressive advertising campaign. In the early 1980s growers were levied a promotion assessment of 15 cents per box. Most of these funds are used to sell Washington apples nationally. The industry budgeted a $4.5 million national advertising campaign for the 1983-84 crop. Included were radio ads in over 70 market areas and on the 1,000 stations in the Paul Harvey network during the September through June period. Both network and local television ads also are important, especially in the major urban markets.

Some experts feel the domestic apple market is nearly saturated and that additional large markets for Washington apples will have to be found overseas. International exports grew from just a few percent in the early '70s to a quarter of all fresh-packed apples by 1980. Taiwan is the state's largest apple export customer followed by Canada, Saudi Arabia, and Hong Kong. Big Delicious Washington apples are considered dessert and gift apples in most foreign lands and may sell for a dollar or more apiece. This limits demand in the world's developing countries, but doesn't explain the lack of sales in Japan, viewed by industry experts as a potentially huge market.

Japan has imposed a complete quarantine on Pacific Northwest apples, some of which are infested with codling moth larvae. Japan is free of this pest and has even refused test shipments for fear that imports might contaminate their domestic fruit. Researchers are testing fumigation and irradiation methods to eliminate the pest. But even larvae-free apples might not be able to crack the Japanese market. Some think the real problem is political, the result of a strong lobbying effort by Japan's 95,000 apple growers. With inefficient, tiny orchards that average just 1.3 acres, they evidently fear competition from Eastern Washington apples.

*In Eastern Washington, fruit labels are considered regional art. Modern packing methods have eliminated wooden crates, but old fruit-box labels remain collector's items. They can be seen in area museums and purchased in Northwest antique stores. With permission of H.S. Denison & Company*

*Opposite page: Early morning sun rises and fog lifts over Spokane, Eastern Washington's metropolis.*

*Right: Riverfront Wenatchee with fruit storage warehouse in foreground.*

*Below: Port of Pasco  John Alwin photos*

# CITYSCAPES

Although Eastern Washington is an agricultural region, not everyone lives down on the farm or in tiny hamlets with just a general store and gas station. In fact, 75 percent of residents live within the region's three Bureau of the Census defined metropolitan areas, and an additional 10 percent live within its five other communities of 10,000 or more.

Each of Eastern Washington's larger communities has its own unique history and personality, and presents a cityscape all its own. Historic and mature Walla Walla with its stately tree-lined residential streets; long-established and Western Ellensburg, home to an annual rodeo extravaganza; sunny Yakima with its intensely loyal citizenry; somewhat off-the-beaten-path Wenatchee, Washington's apple capital, picturesquely nestled at the base of the Cascade ramparts; the young and fast-growing "Desert Oasis Town" of Moses Lake; the burgeoning Tri-Cities, riverside communities synonymous with commerce and science; curious and isolated Pullman, literally and figuratively dominated by hilltop Washington State University; and urban, though not urbane, Spokane, this homey, friendly-people hub of a vast inland empire.

Following is a photo essay, a picture portrait, of each of these largest of Eastern Washington communities.

A

B

# WALLA WALLA

H

Whitman College,
Walla Walla, Washington

G

(A) Historic, mature Walla Walla has many fine, older homes along Palouse and Boyer. John Alwin photo  (B) Old Fort Walla Walla, formerly Nez Perce, west of town on the Columbia predates the city by decades. The site of this HBC fur trade post now lies at the bottom of Lake Wallula. Lithograph from Pacific Railroad Survey, 1853  (C) Fair time in the town with the rhythmic Indian name. John Alwin photo (D) One of many graves at the site of the military's Fort Walla Walla on the city's west side. John Alwin photo  (E) The Great Grave and monument at nearby Whitman Mission National Historic Site. John Alwin photo  (F) Downtown Walla Walla, view north up Second Avenue from Alder. Landmark Marcus Whitman Towers in distance. John Alwin photo  (G) Picture postcard of Whitman College mailed September 12, 1913. The college began as Whitman Seminary in 1859, the same year the town got its name. University of Washington Library photo  (H) Memorial Building on Whitman campus, the state's oldest college and one of its most highly regarded. John Alwin photo

C

F

E

D

113

A

B

# ELLENSBURG

C

K

J

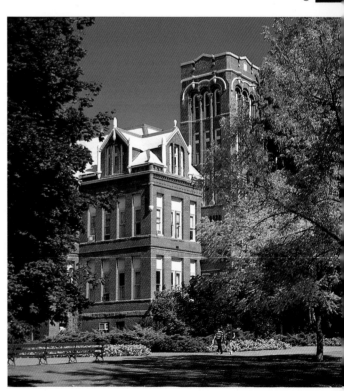

*(A) The Ellensburg Rodeo, a 60-year tradition. John Alwin photo    (B) 1890 view from Capitol Hill, now Craig's Hill, looking west down Third from the Chestnut intersection. Large building at left, now the Castle Apartments, was built in 1889 as a prospective governor's mansion in an effort to sell Ellensburg as the state capitol. Haynes Foundation Collection, Montana Historical Society    (C) Rossow's U-Tote-Em, home of the Ellensburger. John Alwin photo    (D) Gerry Williams pours salmon eggs at Pautzke Bait Company, one of Ellensburg's 30 manufacturers. John Alwin photo    (E) Midway at the Kittitas County Fair. John Alwin photo    (F) Jagged Stewart Range forms an impressive backdrop to this rainshadow town. John Alwin photo    (G) Former Ellensburg residents return whenever possible to the Labor Day weekend festivities. John Alwin photo (H) Yakima Indians in native regalia are always a favorite in the annual Rodeo Parade. John Alwin photo (I) Ninety-year-old Barge Hall on the campus at Central.    (J) The cornerstone of downtown's National Historic District, the Davidson Block, was under construction when the devastating July 4, 1889 fire leveled the central business district. John Alwin photo    (K) Non-stop action at the carnival. John Alwin photo*

115

# YAKIMA

A

B

N. P. Depot and Park, North Yakima, Wash.

H

G

C

D

(A) West down Yakima Avenue, the heart of Eastern Washington's second largest city. John Alwin photo   (B) Burlington Northern and Union Pacific yards from Nob Hill overpass, central business district looms in distance. John Alwin photo   (C) Boise Cascade mill draws its lumber from the forested Cascades to the west. John Alwin photo   (D) Apples are coated by the truckload prior to storage at Yakima's famous Fruit Row, a mile-long warehouse district west of downtown. John Alwin photo   (E) With M-16 at the ready, Sergeant Patrick Maloney stands guard at Headquarters Company, 15th Engineering Battalion during Operation Caber Toss on 263,000-acre Yakima Firing Center just north of the city. John Alwin photo   (F) Youthful queen at the 13th annual Indian Days Celebration on the Yakima Indian Reservation adjacent to suburban Yakima. John Alwin photo   (G) North Yakima, after 1917 simply Yakima, took form along the Northern Pacific tracks in the mid-1880s. This view shows North Front Street looking south in 1886. Yakima Valley Historical Museum photo.   (H) Picture postcard mailed from North Yakima, April 5, 1906. University of Washington Library photo

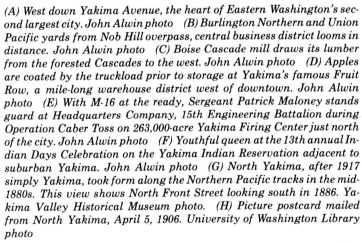

F

E

117

# WENATCHEE

A

B

G

(A) Lunch break on the lawn in front of the Chelan County Courthouse. John Alwin photo  (B) With the Columbia at its foot and the Cascades as a backdrop, few Eastern Washington communities can rival Wenatchee's setting. Fruit warehouses line the river bank. John Alwin photo  (C) Cheap and abundant hydroelectric power lured Alcoa Aluminum to Wenatchee in the 1950s. With more than 900 workers, the Alcoa plant is Wenatchee's largest employer. John Alwin photo (D) Although a bit off the beaten path, Wenatchee is one of Eastern Washington's largest cities with more than 17,000 residents. John Alwin photo  (E) Wenatchee-based Denison & Co. used this colorful fruit label picturing founder H. S. Denison's daughter, Lois, from 1921 into the 1940s. With permission of H.S. Denison & Company  (F) View of the city from beautiful Ohme Gardens north of town. John Alwin photo  (G) Wenatchee developed as an early center for steamboat travel on the Columbia. Some would like to see navigation opened once again between the Tri-Cities and Wenatchee. North Central Washington Museum photo

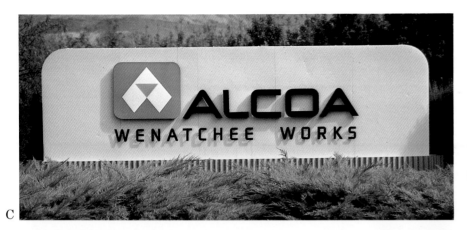

C

D

F

E

# MOSES LAKE

A

G

F

B

C

E

D

*(A) Moses Lake is one of Eastern Washington's newest communities. Formerly hamlet-size Neppel, it was incorporated in 1938 and acquired its present name. (B) Water towers take on added importance in this dry country. (C) Although in a near-desert, this golf course is as green as any west of the mountains. (D) Residents along North Shore Drive avail themselves of the amenities on Parker Horn. (E) Hardly anything keeps Jim away from his favorite fishing spot on the I-90 bridge next to Moses Lake State Park. (F) Japan Airlines pilots ready for take-off at the Grant County Airport. (G) Control tower at this former military air base, now one of the busiest airports in the nation and internationally famous as a jet crew training center. John Alwin photos*

121

# TRI-CITIES
## Pasco — Kennewick — Richland

A

B

G

(A) The "300 Area" laboratory complex on the Department of Energy's Hanford Site beside the Columbia just north of Richland. Activities are geared largely to advanced nuclear research and development. U.S. Department of Energy photo  (B) The "Blue" bridge spanning the Columbia River between Kennewick and Pasco is symbolic of the links between the Tri-Cities. John Alwin photo  (C) Unloading containerized cargo at busy Port of Pasco. John Alwin photo  (D) Food processing is an important part of the Tri-Cities economy. John Alwin photo  (E) 1944 photo 'B' Reactor at Hanford, one of the major sources for plutonium which produced fuel for the bomb dropped on Nagasaki. U.S. Department of Energy photo  (F) Futuristic, Fast Flux Test Facility is the prime U.S. Testing center for breeder reactor technology. U.S. Department of Energy photo  (G) Where it all began for the Tri-Cities. This 1884 view is of the Northern Pacific Railroad construction town of Ainsworth, which sprouted at the junction of the Columbia and Snake rivers near present-day Sacajawea State Park. Washington State University Library photo

C

F

E

D

# PULLMAN

A

G

(A) Hilltop Washington State University looms over Pullman both literally and figuratively. Its 16,000 students constitute a majority of the town's population. John Alwin photo   (B) Pullman's still important agricultural base is evident. John Alwin photo   (C) The clock tower of WSU's Bryan Hall. John Alwin photo   (D) Three graduating seniors relax in Ferry Hall dorm. Washington State University Library photo   (E) WSU's Cougars bring big-league college sports to the Palouse. WSU Athletic Department photo   (F) A large percentage of WSU students live in on-campus housing. Surprisingly, King County contributes more than twice as many students as any other county. John Alwin photo   (G) WSU cadets on parade, July 1898. Washington State University Library photo

B

C

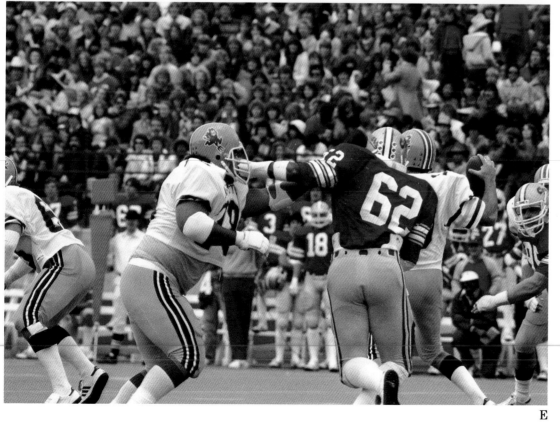

D

F

E

125

A

B

C

# SPOKANE

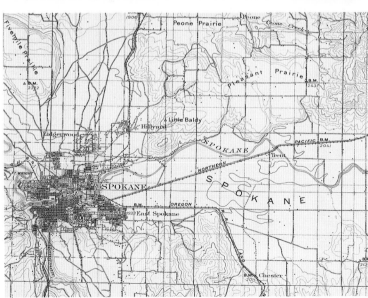

J

I

126

D

E

F

30 - Sprague Avenue, West from Howard, Spokane, Washington.

(A) View down Washington Street from the South Hill. Landmark Paulsen Center, the city's first skyscraper dominates this end of the central business district. John Alwin photo    (B) The Great Northern Tower, symbol of Spokane and focal point for Riverside Park on the site of Expo '74. John Alwin photo    (C) Contrary to popular misconceptions held west of the Cascades, the Spokane garden club does not grow sagebrush. Gardens in Manito Park, one of almost 100 operated by the city and country. John Alwin photo (D) North down Wall from Riverside. Downtown remains a vibrant, personable environment. The convenient skywalk links a 10-block area. John Alwin photo    (E) One of the many B-52 Stratofortress bombers stationed at nearby Fairchild Air Force Base. John Alwin photo    (F) Travelling musicians stop at Riverside Park to test Cajun music on locals. John Alwin photo    (G) Mayor Jim Chase sometimes accuses western Washingtonians of launching probes to test for life east of the mountains. John Alwin photo (H) Penny postcard dated Spokane, January 11, 1907. University of Washington Library photo    (I) St. John's Episcopal Cathedral rises above fall colors on the South Hill. John Alwin photo    (J) Spokane as it was, 1898. U.S. Geological Survey, Spokane Quadrangle

H

G

A

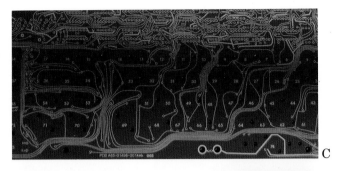

B

C

D

F

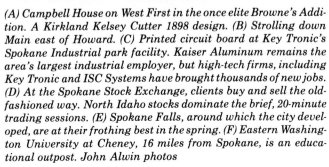

E

*(A) Campbell House on West First in the once elite Browne's Addition. A Kirkland Kelsey Cutter 1898 design. (B) Strolling down Main east of Howard. (C) Printed circuit board at Key Tronic's Spokane Industrial park facility. Kaiser Aluminum remains the area's largest industrial employer, but high-tech firms, including Key Tronic and ISC Systems have brought thousands of new jobs. (D) At the Spokane Stock Exchange, clients buy and sell the old-fashioned way. North Idaho stocks dominate the brief, 20-minute trading sessions. (E) Spokane Falls, around which the city developed, are at their frothing best in the spring. (F) Eastern Washington University at Cheney, 16 miles from Spokane, is an educational outpost. John Alwin photos*